W9-AHC-027
LOVELESS
愛

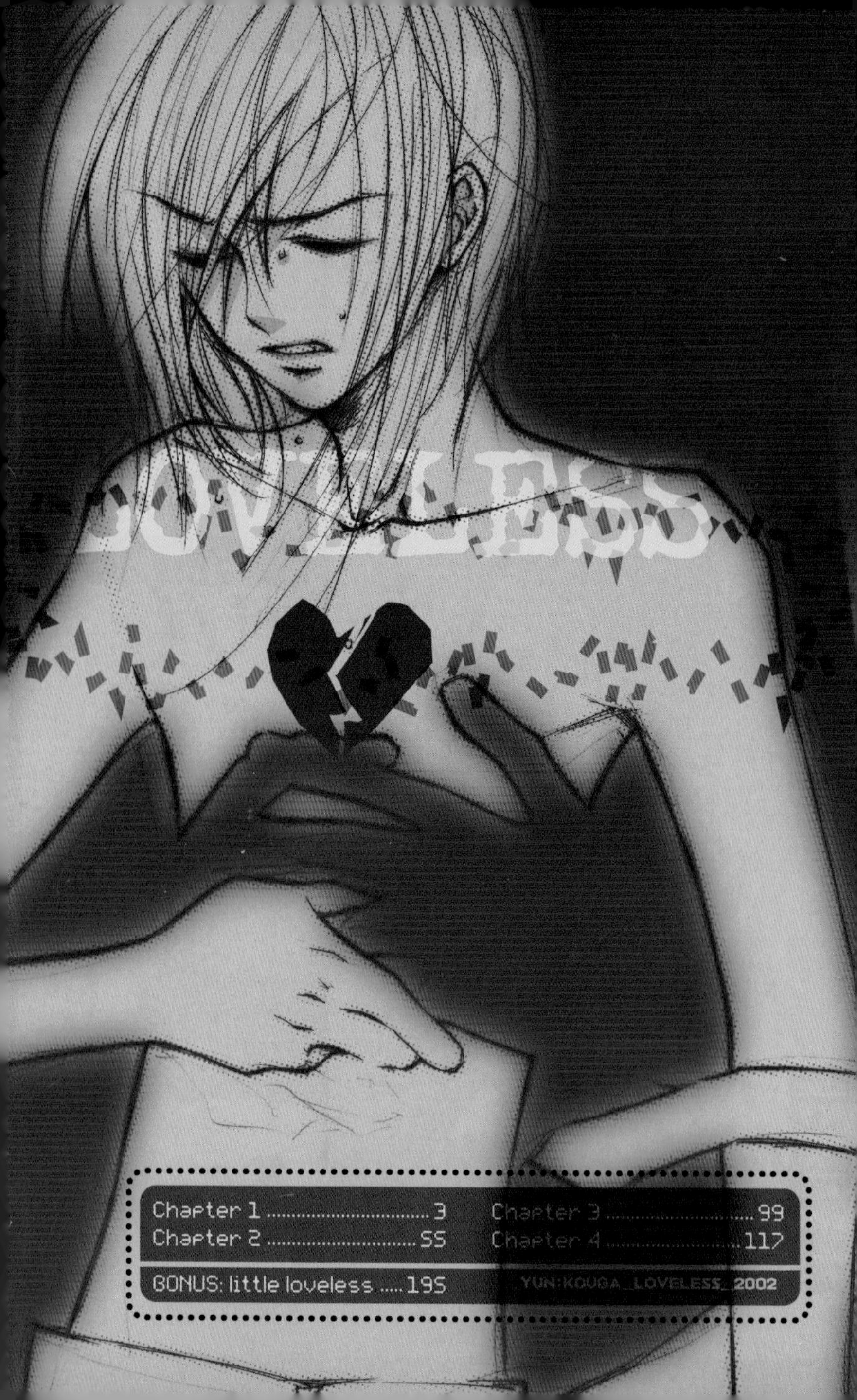
LOVELESS

"I'M GOING TO TELL YOU A SECRET. SOMETHING FOR YOUR EARS ONLY—
MY REAL NAME."
FLICK
BELOVED.
ONE WHO IS ADORED.
"DON'T FORGET."
AS IF I COULD EVER FORGET WHEN ERASURE IS THE THING I FEAR MOST.
HOW COULD I FORGET?
Huh?
For me?
Just me?
BDMP
BDMP
ONE WEEK AFTER I HEARD THAT BEAUTIFUL NAME...
...SEIMEI...
YOU WON'T.
...WAS DEAD.

CHAPTER 1

LOVE

(I WONDERED WHAT HE MEANT BY "REAL NAME," BUT...)
IT WAS FITTING, SINCE EVERYONE LOVED SEIMEI.
BUT SEIMEI DIED.
HE DIED IN AN UNIMAGINABLE WAY.
HE WAS MURDERED.

GOOD MORNING.
CHAK
I'M RITSUKA AOYAGI.

KTUNK
OH!
OH, GOOD MORNING. ♡
YOU'RE AOYAGI?
HI.
UM, WHERE ARE YOUR PARENTS?

SMILE
THEY COULDN'T MAKE IT.
THEY'RE BUSY PEOPLE.

HUH?
B...
BUSY? BUT...
THIS IS YOUR FIRST DAY AS A TRANSFER STUDENT...
I BROUGHT MY OWN PAPERWORK.
YOU CAME BY YOURSELF...?
SIXTH GRADERS CAN GET TO SCHOOL ON THEIR OWN.
THAT'S NORMAL.
FLICK
FLICK

DON'T WORRY.
I'M USED TO THIS.
OH.
MS. SHINO-NOME.
AO-YAGI...
PLENTY OF KIDS COME FROM HOMES LIKE MINE.
IT DOESN'T BOTHER ME.
MY HOME-ROOM IS NUMBER 3, RIGHT?
LET'S GO!
SHKLAK
OH!
EXCUSE US!
AOYAGI!
HE'S SUCH A...
...STRONG YOUNG BOY.
MURMUR
YES, AND...
HE HAS A BIT OF A PAST.
YANO JONAN ELEMENTARY SCHOOL
RITSUKA AOYAGI
SAYING HE'S USED TO IT AND ALL.
HOW SO?
THERE ARE TROUBLING COMMENTS IN THE FILE FROM HIS OLD SCHOOL.
YOU WON'T BELIEVE THEM.
MURMUR
OH MY!
MUR
THAT WAS IN THE NEWS.
OH, THAT!

RITSUKA AOYAGI.
SAME AOYAGI AS THAT INCIDENT.
YANO JONAN ELEMENTARY SCHOOL
RITSUKA AOYAGI
POOR BOY, I HOPE HE'S NOT TRAUMATIZED.
AND THOSE BRUISES...

HE'LL TAKE A DELICATE TOUCH.
CAN MS. SHINO-NOME HANDLE THIS?
SHE'S A LITTLE... WELL... YOU KNOW.

NOVEMBER 17

RITSUKA

•Daily Duties:
Sakurada, Tayama

AOYAGI

This week's goals:
Memorize script

SAY HELLO TO RITSUKA AOYAGI!
HI.
NICE TO MEET YOU.
WOW!
RITSUKA? HE'S SO COOL!!
WHAT-EVER.
LOOKS AVERAGE TO ME.
PING!
HEY, YUIKO. WHY DON'TCHA TALK TO HIM LATER?
WHAT?
OKAY!
LET'S BEGIN!
START FROM PAGE 46 OF YOUR TEXT-BOOKS.
NO!
YUIKO'S TOO SHY!!
THEN WHY'D YOU SHOUT ABOUT HIM BEING COOL?
ERGH—
NO!

BLUSH
N...
WOW... HUGE BOOBS.
Looks...
...kinda dumb.
HI.

HE'S...
HE'S SITTING NEXT TO ME!!
CAN I SEE YOUR TEXTBOOK?
She's a weirdo.
SKRUT
H...
HERE!!
WHAM
'KAY.
For me?
We could just share...
UH...
SOMETHING...
GOTTA SAY SOMETHING!
BDMP BDMP BDMP
SQRM
HEY, RITSUKA, DO YOU HAVE A CELL PHONE?
...
NO.
I DON'T.
What?

TALK...
OH.
'KAY.
WELL THEN...
GOTTA TALK!!
UH, WHERE'S YOUR CRAM SCHOOL?
DON'T GO TO ONE.
HUH?
OH, THEN...
WHO'S YOUR FAVORITE IN MORNING MUSUME?
GOTTA TALK!
YUIKO LIKES GOMAKI!
She's so cute.

THERE'S TOO MANY. I CAN'T TELL THEM APART.
WHAAAT?
FLICK
NO WAY.
YOU DON'T KNOW MO-MUSU?
HEE HEE HEE HEE
LOOK.
WHY ARE YOU INTER-ROGATING ME?
HUH?
BECAUSE EVERYONE TOLD YUIKO TO TALK TO YOU.
FLAIL FLAIL FLAIL
HUH?
THEN WHY ASK ABOUT STUFF LIKE THAT?
OH! WELL, YOU'RE SO COOL!
YUIKO THINKS EVERYONE WANTS TO GET TO KNOW YOU BETTER.
THAT SO?
A moron for sure.
SO I'M "COOL"?
BLUSH
YOU DUMMY! WE DIDN'T SAY THAT!
YOU'RE THE ONE WHO SAID HE WAS COOL!
GYAAH
NO!
GRR
ALL OF YOU!
WAH
STOP!
IT'S THE MIDDLE OF CLASS!
PEOPLE WHO GET USED BY OTHERS...
SKRUT

...ARE PATHETIC.
PEOPLE WHO USE OTHERS ARE DUMB, BUT NOT AS DUMB AS THE ONES WHO GET USED.
H-USH...
...
SO YOU THINK ...
...YUIKO'S DUMB?
SOB
I HATE DUMB GIRLS.
HERE'S YOUR BOOK.
FWAP
SIXTH GRADE JAPANESE
PLIP
SIXTH GRADE JAPANESE
WAAAAH!!
CRASH
GYAH!!
I CAN'T BELIEVE HIM!
WHAT A JERK!
GYA
GYA
GYA
POOR YUIKO!
HOW COULD YOU MAKE A GIRL CRY?!
HEY, EVERYONE! IT'S CLASS TIME!!
CLASS!!

UNREAL...
DAY ONE AND HE'S ALREADY TURNED ALL THE GIRLS AGAINST HIM.
HE'S EITHER AWESOME...
...OR TOTALLY LAME!!
THE WORLD IS FULL OF PREDATORY PEOPLE.
THEY PRETEND TO BE YOUR FRIEND BUT TREAT YOU LIKE A SLAVE.
SEIMEI, LIFE SUCKS.
I WISH...
...IT WOULD HURRY UP AND END.
RITSUKA!
RITSUKA!

HEY, RITSUKA!
LUNCH TIME!
DON'T BOTHER WITH HIM, YUIKO!
HE'S A CREEP!
GRR
GRR
GRR
EHEH...
LET'S EAT TOGETHER.
CLAK
That jerk! Ignore him!
YOUR FRIENDS WON'T LIKE IT IF YOU HANG AROUND ME.
WHAT? THAT'S NOT TRUE!
FLOP
Eheh.
Yeah, it is.
YUIKO LOVES FRIED BREAD!
WHAT DO YOU LIKE TO EAT FOR LUNCH, RITSUKA?
WHAT-EVER.
HERE I WAS, ENJOYING SOME PEACE AND QUIET... HOW OBNOXIOUS.
Sigh...
CHEWING'S A HASSLE, SO I LIKE SOFT STUFF.
HUH? REALLY?
THAT'S LIKE A GRANDPA.
Grandpa?!
LOOK.
DON'T GO OUT OF YOUR WAY TO TALK TO ME.

IT'S A HASSLE TO ANSWER ALL THESE QUESTIONS.
BLUSH
What a creep!
RITSUKA.
YOU...
YOU REALLY DON'T EVEN TRY, DO YOU?
NOPE.
I DON'T.
EXCUSE ME.
WHAT TIME DOES SCHOOL LET OUT?
IT'S SATURDAY, SO THEY END AT 12:30.
THANK YOU.
IT'LL LOOK QUESTION-ABLE ...
BUT WAITING OUTSIDE THE SCHOOL GATE IS THE SUREST BET.

FFFT
BING
BONG

BING
BONG
RITSUKA!
GOING HOME?
DOING ANY-THING?
I'VE GOT NO PLANS, SO I'M GOING TO THE LIBRARY.
WHAT? THE SCHOOL LIBRARY?
ELEMENTARY SCHOOLS DON'T HAVE ANY GOOD BOOKS.
SO I'M GOING TO A *LIBRARY*.
A PUBLIC ONE. FOR ADULTS.
REALLY?!
YUIKO WANTS TO COME!
PING!
WE'RE GOING HOME. WHAT ARE YOU DOING, YUIKO?
CARRY MY BAGS!
HEY!
SORRY, NOT TODAY.
YUIKO'S GOING HOME WITH RITSUKA.
What?
You weren't invited!
GRR—
GRR
WHAT'S ALL THAT ABOUT?
GRR
GRR
YUIKO'S PISSING ME OFF!
LOOK.
IF YOU KEEP THIS UP, THEY'RE GOING TO TURN ON YOU.
IT'S FINE! THEY'RE YUIKO'S FRIENDS.
AND IT'S NOT "LOOK," IT'S *YUIKO*.

YUIKO HAWATARI!
SMILE ♥
JUST CALL ME YUIKO!!
NO THANKS.
Why are idiots so happy?
WHAT? HUH?
WHY? WHY?
WHY NOT? SAY YUIKO!
SAY IT!
SAY IT!
No way.
AO-YAGI!
TRMBL
MS. SHINO-NOME?
H...
HOW WAS YOUR FIRST DAY?
I'M ALWAYS HERE TO LISTEN.
Huh?!
OH...
YOU KNOW ABOUT ME NOW, DON'T YOU?
I'M FINE.
HAWATARI HERE IS BEING SUPER NICE TO ME.

REALLY?
THAT'S NICE OF YOU, HAWATARI.
Ah...
OKAY!
WE'RE GONNA GO TO THE LIBRARY NOW.
HUH?
OH.
OKAY!
HUH?
WHAT?
RIT-SUKA!
YOU'RE SUCH A FAKER!

WELL, EXCUSE ME FOR BEING A FAKE!
I JUST CAN'T STAND PEOPLE WORRYING ABOUT ME.
YOU'RE SO WEIRD!
HEE
HEE
IT'S LIKE YOU'VE GOT A SPLIT PERSONALITY, RITSUKA.

BADUMP

HUH?
UM.
SORRY, RITSUKA!
YUIKO'S ...!
SOR...
DON'T EVER SAY THAT AGAIN!
LEAVE ME ALONE.
GO AWAY!
ZING
!
DON'T SAY THAT...
RITSUKA!
DASH
Y...
YUIKO DOESN'T GET IT, BUT...
SPLIT PERSONALITY?
SORRY!
IT'S NOT LIKE THAT. I'M...

WHAT'S THE MATTER, RITSUKA?
WHY ARE YOU CRYING?
TUG

WHA ...?!
YOU.
I'M NOT CRYING, YOU JERK!
WHO'S CRYING?!
GRRRK
LET GO OF MY ARM!
WHO THE HELL ARE YOU?!
YOU DON'T KNOW ME?
WHY SHOULD I?
LET ME GO!
YOU NEVER CAME FOR ME, RITSUKA.
SO I CAME FOR YOU INSTEAD.
WHOA...
THIS GUY...
FLICK

HE DOESN'T HAVE EARS.
RIP
LET GO OF ME!
HOW DO YOU KNOW MY NAME?
HISS
WHO ARE YOU?!
HISS
He's an adult.
A KIDNAPPER?!
A PERVERT?!
HISS
He gives me the creeps!
HE'S AN ADULT!!
NOT VERY TRUSTING, IS HE?
I'M A FIGHTER.
HUH?!
Sounds fishy.
HISS HISS
WELL... THIS IS AWKWARD.
SEIMEI NEVER TOLD YOU...
...ABOUT ME?

YOU'RE SEIMEI'S ...
YOU KNEW MY BROTHER ?
YOU'RE SEIMEI'S FRIEND?
BUT YOU NEVER CAME BY OUR HOUSE, RIGHT? I'D HAVE REMEMBERED THAT.
OH...
YES.
WHAT'S YOUR NAME?
SOUBI.
YOU CAME TO SEE ME, SOUBI?
Yes.
BUT WHY?

HEY, ARE YOU BUSY RIGHT NOW?

HUG

LET'S GO MAKE SOME MEMORIES!

BLUSH

SHWUF...

LET'S.

WHATEVER YOU WANT, RITSUKA.

AWRIGHT!!

KINU
ALL RIGHT.
OKAY.
SOMYI VS/OPTICAL 4X
f=8-24mm 2.8
SAY CHEESE!
GA PIXELS!
PING!♥
CLICK
THANK YOU, LADY! ♡
OH!
DON'T MENTION IT.
KINUTA PA
AWE-SOME! WE TOOK A TON OF PICTURES.
SO!
THIS IS MAKING MEMORIES?
THAT'S RIGHT. I'LL PRINT THEM LATER.
YOU BETTER NOT THROW THEM OUT, SOUBI!
HUFF
HUFF

THAT SOUNDS LOVELY.
BUT LET'S TALK SOME MORE.
WON'T THAT MAKE FOR BETTER MEMORIES?
NUH-UH!
YOU FORGET WITHOUT PHOTOS. SO WE HAVE TO TAKE PICTURES FIRST.
FWUMP
OTHERWISE YOU'LL JUST FORGET I WAS EVER HERE.
OF COURSE NOT! I WOULD NEVER FORGET.
YOU WILL.
BUT...
IT'S ALL RIGHT.
IT CAN'T BE HELPED.
RIT-SUKA...
JUST WHAT KIND OF KID IS HE...?
I ONLY LEARNED HIS NAME AND HIS FACE.
HE'S SEIMEI'S BROTHER.

IT'S POINTLESS ...
...TO TRY TO MAKE MEMORIES WITH A STRANGER.
BUT SOUBI, YOU'RE SEIMEI'S FRIEND.
SONY
TO ME...
...THAT COUNTS FOR A LOT!
HM?
OH.
MY EARS ?
...
BUT...
I NEVER KNEW.
THAT SEIMEI ...
...HAD AN ADULT FRIEND.
BLUSH
DON'T WORRY. I WON'T DO ANYTHING TO YOU.

I DON'T BELIEVE YOU!
SCREW YOU, SOUBI!
HNGGH
IT WAS JUST A KISS.
YOU SAID YOU WOULDN'T DO ANY-THING!
YOU SAID...
...NOT ANY-THING!

LEND ME YOUR STRENGTH.
FROM NOW ON, THE TWO OF US...

...MUST BE JOINED BY A DEEP BOND, A BOND STRONGER THAN ANY OTHER PAIR.
STRONG.
DEEP.
STOP IT, YOU CAN'T...
BOND?
WORDS LIKE THAT MAKE MY HEAD SPIN.
!
FLINCH

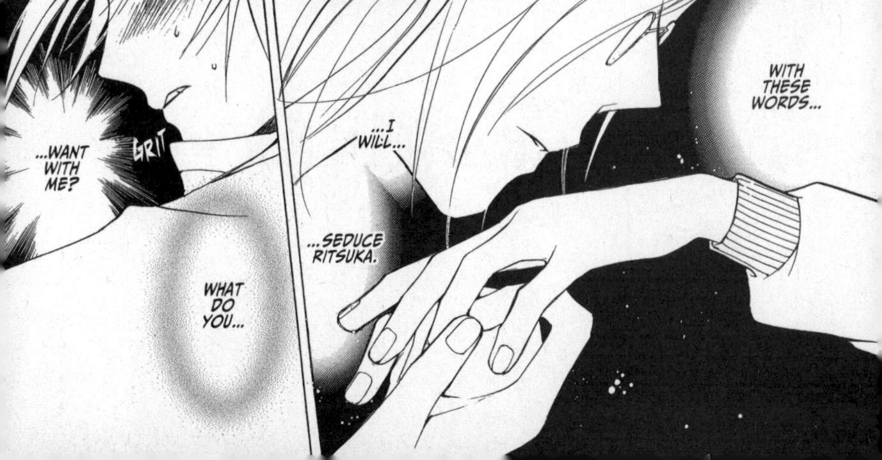
WITH THESE WORDS...
...I WILL...
...SEDUCE RITSUKA.
GRIT
WHAT DO YOU...
...WANT WITH ME?

SOME-ONE'S HERE.
A FIGHTER OTHER THAN MYSELF.
VWOOOSH
THEY'RE CLOSE. SOMEWHERE IN THIS PARK.
WAH!
AI?!
VWEEEN

WE'VE MADE CONTACT.
SHAAAA
ARE YOU OKAY?
YEAH... WE KINDA RAN INTO THEM.
THEY'RE HERE, REALLY CLOSE BY.
RAN INTO THEM?
WH...
WHAT NOW?
DOES...
DOES THAT MEAN YOU WANT TO HAVE SEX?

NOT NOW.
GTAK
I COULDN'T GET HARD FOR A CHILD, RITSUKA.
IT'D BE A PROBLEM IF YOU COULD!!
MY MOM WOULD FAINT IF I LOST MY EARS AT MY AGE.
But you kissed me.
That better be the truth.
I heard you say it.
VWIP
VWIP
THERE'S A FIGHTER HERE!!
I HAVEN'T PREPARED RITSUKA YET. WHAT SHOULD I DO?
THERE'S A FIGHTER HERE!!
WHAT ?!
DOES THIS MEAN WE HAVE TO DO BATTLE? WE WERE JUST TOLD TO BRING HIM IN.
NO ONE SAID ANYTHING ABOUT THIS!
THAT KID HAS A FIGHTER WITH HIM, I KNOW IT.
AND HE'S...
...REALLY BIG!

HE'S HERE!!
I LOVE YOU...
RITSUKA.
HUH?
WHA ...?!
TWITCH
AND HE'S REALLY ...
...POWER-FUL!
Don't ...
EXCUSE ME?!
...jerk me around!
I LOVE YOU.
HEH
I'LL PROTECT YOU.
I'LL DO ANYTHING FOR YOU, RITSUKA.
ANY-THING ...?
SHIVER..
ANY-THING!
I GIVE YOU ALL OF ME.

THEY'RE COMING.
MY BODY.
MY HEART.
MY SOUL.
EVERYTHING FOR YOU.
I'D EVEN GIVE YOU MY LIFE.
I'LL FIGHT FOR YOU, RITSUKA.
SO THERE'S NOTHING TO BE AFRAID OF.
"AFRAID"? OF WHAT?
HOW CAN YOU...
BLUSH
...SAY STUFF LIKE THAT?
I CAN SAY IT...
ALMOST THERE.
...BECAUSE I CAN CAST SPELLS WITH MY WORDS!

WHO THE HELL ARE YOU?

ZSSH

I AM.

YOU!

DON'T TELL ME YOU'RE LOVELESS' FIGHTER!

YOU'RE STILL ALIVE ?!

SOUBI ?!

I WON'T HAND OVER RITSUKA.
BELOVED
BELOVED
"I'LL TELL YOU A SECRET."
BELOVED
SOUBI...
WHAT WERE YOU TO SEIMEI?
YOU...

I AM THE FIGHTER FOR BELOVED.
BELOVED
AND NOW I AM YOURS, RITSUKA.
KNOCK IT OFF! YOU'RE CRAZY!
A FIGHTER CAN'T SERVE TWO MASTERS.
WHAT, SINCE BELOVED IS DEAD, NOW YOU'RE GOING TO SERVE LOVELESS?
THAT'S NOT ALLOWED!
What's going on?
RIT-SUKA.
Someone explain...
FLICK
DON'T WORRY.
I'LL EXPLAIN LATER.
SOUBI.
HE'S SO STRANGE.
ALL THIS IS SO STRANGE.
I CAN'T MAKE SENSE OF IT!...

SO WHY...?
ALL HE DID WAS CALL MY NAME...
...AND I'M CRYING.
LOOK WHAT HE'S DONE!
MIDORI, LET ME FIGHT!
HE'S GOT ZERO PRIDE! I CAN'T FORGIVE HIM!
I KNOW. GO AHEAD!
AFTER ALL, THIS IS OUR DUTY.
I DECLARE ...
...A BATTLE BY WORD SPELL.
HE'S MAKING HIS MOVE.
GO.
I ACCEPT!
WE WILL BE ON AUTO-MATIC.
WHAT?!

HUH?
ON AUTO?
ARE YOU...
...MOCKING US?!
EXPAND...
BATTLE SYSTEMS.
VWEEN
AUTOMATIC MEANS...
...ONLY THE FIGHTER BATTLES.
IN OTHER WORDS, IT'S TWO AGAINST ONE.
FINE THEN!
NOW I'M ANGRY!
IF YOU THINK YOU CAN OWN THE NAME ALL BY YOURSELF, GO RIGHT AHEAD!
MIDORI, GIVE ME YOUR HAND!
WE ARE OF THE SAME SOUL.
WE SHARE THE SAME NAME: BREATHLESS.
I'M NOT...
...MOCKING THEM.

IT'S JUST...
RITSUKA'S NOT READY TO FIGHT YET.
BUT...
breath less
VWEEEEN
I PROMISE.
I WILL PROTECT YOU.
JUST CLOSE YOUR EYES.
"BREATH-LESS."
IT MEANS ...
...A FORCE THAT WILL TAKE YOUR BREATH AWAY.
VWEEEN
EXPAND ...
BATTLE SYSTEMS !
WOOON

GWOOOOO
YOU'RE ON!
RIP.
TEAR APART.
FULL DEFENSE MODE.
NONE OF YOUR ATTACKS SHALL REACH ME.
ZHK
ZHK
ZHK
WHOA!
HE'S UP TO FOUR SYLLABLES ALREADY! ALL MY ATTACKS GOT DEFLECTED...
SIMPLE SPELLS WON'T CUT IT!

SHRED.
RIP
RIP
TEAR UP.
DESTROY.
RIP
ZHK
ZHK
IT'S NO USE.
CRUDE SPELLS LIKE THAT WON'T WORK ON ME.
AND NOW...
...SHALL I ATTACK?
MIDORI WILL BE DAMAGED IF I DO.
!!
DON'T LISTEN TO HIM, AI!
YOU CAN'T HESITATE NOW!
I'M YOUR SACRIFICE!
THE WAY THINGS ARE...
I'M SUPPOSED TO BEAR THE DAMAGE! THAT'S HOW THINGS ARE...
...YOU'RE NOT STRONG ENOUGH TO PROTECT MIDORI.

NGH ...!
CALM DOWN, AI.
DON'T LET HIM GET YOU.
HE'S JUST TRYING TO RILE YOU UP.
HEY.
HEY, HEY. HOLD ON.
I DON'T UNDERSTAND WHAT'S GOING ON.
...
YO
INK
WHOA!
RETREAT.
LEAVE THIS PLACE BEHIND.
Yikes!
So lame. Carrying me?!
VWOOOOON
DOES THIS MAKE SOUBI THE BAD GUY...?
IS HE THE VILLAIN HERE?!
HEY!
THAT'S NO FAIR! HE'S RUNNING AWAY?
GRR
GRR
NO WAY!
AWAY TO A PLACE OF SLEEP.
GRR
HOLD ON A MINUTE!
AWAY LIKE TWO LITTLE BIRDS.
HUH?
BIRDS ?!

FWA FWA
FWA
FWA
FWA
YES.
LITTLE BIRDS.
AREN'T THEY?
THOSE TWO, I MEAN.
SO RETREAT MEANT...
BDMP BDMP
BDMP
THEY VANISHED!
YES.
WHEN I'M FIGHTING, I CAN DO JUST ABOUT ANYTHING...
...BUT SINCE I MADE THE FIRST DECLARATION THIS TIME, I COULDN'T RETREAT.
YOU SEE?

D...
D...
DID THEY...
...DIE?
DIE...
HM? OH NO. I JUST SENT THEM HOME.
SO I HAD THEM RETREAT INSTEAD.
It's a secret banishment trick.

SHFF
SHFF
RITSUKA, I LOVE YOU.
YOU'RE ADORABLE.
WHA...
WHAT THE HELL IS THAT ABOUT?!

WHENEVER YOU'RE IN TROUBLE I'LL ALWAYS COME SAVE YOU. REMEMBER THAT.
HE MAY BE AN ADULT, BUT HE'S SO STRANGE.
PUT ME DOWN...
LET ME HOLD YOU JUST A LITTLE LONGER.
My ears!
No biting!

THAT WAS THE FIRST TIME...
...ANYONE'S EVER SAID ANYTHING LIKE THAT TO ME.
RITSUKA, IT'S THOSE EYES.
THEY'RE WHY I'M WILLING TO THROW EVERYTHING AWAY.
PUT ME DOWN.
THOSE EYES FULL OF YEARNING...
EYES THAT CAN FORGIVE ANYTHING.
TMP
HMPH
WELL THEN, SEE YOU.
WHAT?
"See you"?

FWOOO
SOUBI...
HE'S GONE?
SOUBI ?!
WAIT...
REALLY ?!
WHAT ?
BUT...
YOU SAID YOU'D EXPLAIN LATER...
SO EXPLAIN, DAMN IT!
ARGH!
I DON'T BELIEVE THIS!
CRAP! IT'S 6 O'CLOCK ?
I'LL MISS MY CURFEW!
BUT...
EVEN SO...
I STILL HAVE THOSE 50 PHOTOS IN MY DIGITAL CAMERA.
TAK
TAK

SEE...
KREE
KREE
THIS IS WHY I SAID PHOTOS ARE IMPORTANT.
SO, ULTIMATELY...
YOU WERE NOT ABLE TO RETRIEVE LOVELESS, CORRECT?
BUT NOTHING WAS THE WAY YOU SAID IT WOULD BE.
YOU SAID THAT LOVELESS WOULDN'T HAVE A FIGHTER YET.

HE'S A SIXTH GRADER.
I ASSUMED IT WOULD GO SMOOTHLY SINCE YOU'RE THE SAME AGE.
LOVELESS HAD AN INCREDIBLE FIGHTER WITH HIM.
IT WAS SOUBI.
FROM BELOVED.
!
THAT CAN'T BE.
SSHK
IT WAS SOUBI?
I DON'T BELIEVE THAT...
BUT THE NAME IS DIFFERENT.
I WAS PRETTY SHOCKED TOO.
BELOVED DIED, SO HOW COULD HE STILL BE ALIVE?
SKWEEZ
HE'S A DISGRACE TO ALL FIGHTERS.
...
BREATH-LESS?
YES?
YOU KNOW YOU CANNOT BRING A FIGHTER HERE.

NO.
THE TWO OF US GO EVERY-WHERE TOGETHER.
SKWEEZ
...
BREATHLESS, WILL YOU TRY AGAIN?
OR...
OF COURSE WE'LL GO.
IT'S WRONG FOR LOVELESS TO CLAIM A FIGHTER WHO ISN'T HIS.
AND IT'S EVEN MORE WRONG OF SOUBI TO TAKE A SECOND SACRIFICE.
THIS TIME WE'LL GET THE JOB DONE!

TIK
HOW ARE YOU DOING, RITSUKA?
FINE, I GUESS.
TOK
TIK
TOK
TOK
DID ANYTHING HAPPEN ...
...THIS WEEK?
TIK
NOT REALLY.
HEY, DR. KATSUKO.
DO THAT THING.
WHAT THING?
COME ON, YOU KNOW.
THAT HYPNOSIS THING.
HMM...
SKTCH
ALL RIGHT, BUT I DON'T THINK IT WILL WORK THE WAY YOU EXPECT IT TO, RITSUKA.
I KNOW YOU'RE AFRAID.

THE WAY YOU ACT SO TOUGH JUST MASKS...
...HOW SCARED YOU TRULY ARE, RITSUKA.
IF I CAN GO BACK TWO YEARS...
...MAYBE "RITSUKA" WILL SHOW UP.
HE HAS MULTIPLE PERSON-ALITIES?
WHAT ABOUT THE BOY'S MEMORIES?
HOW MANY PERSON-ALITIES ARE WE TALKING ABOUT?
WARD
TO BE SPECIFIC, WE'RE TALKING ABOUT IDENTITIES SWITCHING PLACES.
TWO YEARS AGO ONE IDENTITY VANISHED AND HASN'T RETURNED.
HE ONLY HAS ONES FORMED THESE PAST TWO YEARS.
JUST THIS ONE AND THE "RITSUKA AOYAGI" WHO HE WAS FROM BIRTH TO AGE 10.

YOU'RE INJURED.
YEAH.
SWF
DOES IT HURT?
SURE, I GUESS.
BUT IT'S NOTHING I CAN'T DEAL WITH.
DID YOUR MOTHER DO THAT TO YOU?
THOSE INJURIES MUST BE CHILD ABUSE.
HIS MOTHER IS A COMPLETE HYSTERIC.
BUT THE BOY DOESN'T DISPLAY ANY TROUBLESOME BEHAVIOR.
WERE YOU BULLIED AT SCHOOL?
OF COURSE NOT!!
COME ON, DR. KATSUKO, WHAT ABOUT THE HYPNOSIS?

SO... RITSUKA.
IF "HE" COMES BACK, WHAT WILL YOU DO?

"HE."
...
IF...

IF "RITSUKA" APPEARS, YOU TELL HIM FOR ME...
HE CAN HAVE THIS BODY BACK, SO TAKE IT.
AND YOU'RE FINE WITH THAT?
YEAH.

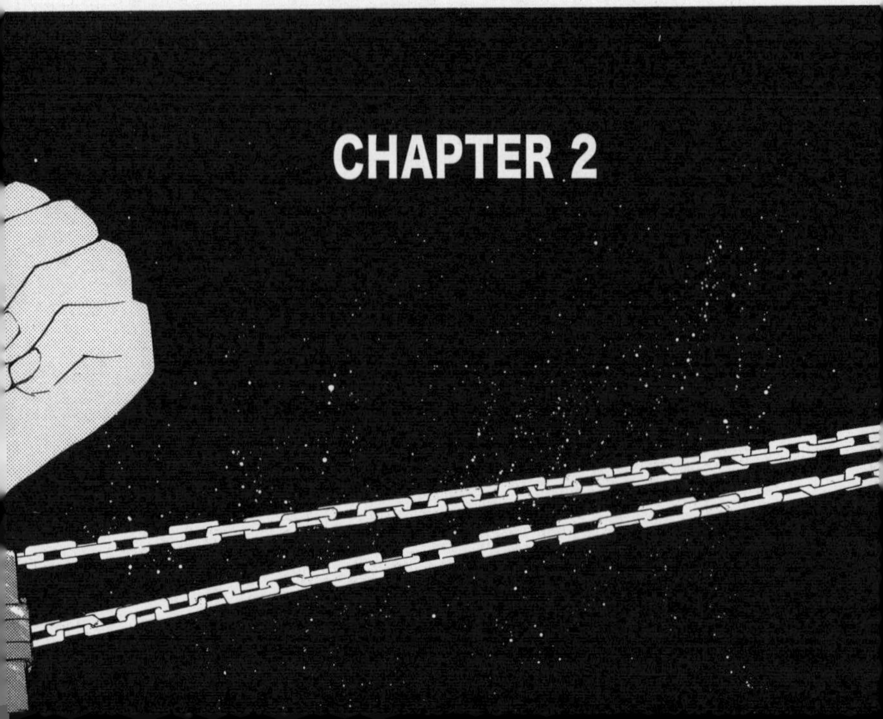

CHAPTER 2

I SUSPECT THIS TO BE A CASE OF AMNESIA RATHER THAN TRUE MULTIPLE PERSONALITIES.

SOME KIND OF SHOCK CAUSED HIS OLD MEMORIES TO BE LOST, WHILE SIMULTANEOUSLY...

BUT YOU SAID HIS PERSONALITY CHANGED.

HIS MOTHER IS THE PROBLEM.

SHE INSISTS THAT HE'S "NOT HER SON," WHICH HAS AN UNDERSTANDABLY POWERFUL EFFECT ON THE BOY.

MOM IS WAITING FOR "RITSUKA"...

HE'S REACHING THE LIMITS OF HIS ABILITY TO NAVIGATE THIS TENSION.

I DOUBT HE CAN MAINTAIN HIS SENSE OF SELF, LIVING LIKE THAT...

TIME'S UP.
THAT'S ALL FOR TODAY.
BOW
OKAY.
THANK YOU!
HEY, RITSUKA?
YES?
SKRUT
HOW ABOUT WE GO ON A DATE?

HUH?
I'M DONE FOR THE DAY. SO LET'S GO! ♡
WHATEVER YOU LIKE, IT'S MY TREAT!
What?
Date?
A date!
Yeah!

I CAN'T. MY CURFEW IS SIX.
I wanna go... ...on a date.
Crud. I wanna go!
AH WELL. TOO BAD... I SUPPOSE.
Yeah, too bad.
YOU KNOW, I LIKE YOU THE WAY YOU ARE NOW.
BUT MY MOTHER DOESN'T.
RITSUKA... THIS MAY BE HARD FOR YOU TO UNDER-STAND.
BUT IT'S OKAY FOR PEOPLE TO LIVE THEIR LIVES FOR THEMSELVES.
...
DR. KATSUKO!!
THAT'S...
THAT'S...
THANK YOU VERY MUCH...
...IMPOSSIBLE...
DOCTOR! WILL YOU TAKE A PICTURE WITH ME?
TA-DA!
YEAH! LET'S DO IT!!
YAY!!
IT'S NOT LIKE I THINK IT'S A BAD THING.

IT'S NOT LIKE I THINK THAT "BEING MYSELF" IS A BAD THING, REALLY...

BUT...

I'M HOME.
IN MY CASE...
Good, it's six.
I made it!
CHAK
Whew!
RITSUKA?
TMP TMP
WELCOME HOME!

THE FACT THAT I'M NOT "RITSUKA"...
TMP
YOU'RE LATE. I WAS SO...
...WORRIED.
TMP

...IS A SIN.
BDMP BDMP
HOW WAS IT? IS THE THERAPY WORKING?
I'M THE ONLY ONE WHO DOESN'T REMEMBER "RITSUKA."
I'M SORRY.
SO RITSUKA.
YOU'VE COME BACK TO ME, HAVEN'T YOU?
RITSUKA?
I'M STILL ...
...NOT ...
...SO I CAN'T EVEN PRETEND.
!!
...
SHAKE
SHAKE...

NGH...
WHY...?
WHERE DID RITSUKA GO?
SOB
RITSUKA ...
SOB
NGH ...!
"IT'S OKAY TO LIVE YOUR LIFE FOR YOURSELF."
BUT DR. KATSUKO, HOW CAN I DO THAT?
HOW COULD I EVER LEAVE MY MOTHER WHEN SHE'S SO SAD?
I DON'T GET IT, DR. KATSUKO.
CHOMP
HOW AM I SUPPOSED TO LIVE FOR MYSELF?
HHCK!

WHO ARE YOU? YOU'RE NOT RITSUKA!
GIVE ME BACK MY RITSUKA!!
...
She bit me.
Wasn't on my guard.
STING STING
WHAT ARE YOU DOING HERE?!
WHAP
MISAKI!
WHY DO YOU HAVE RITSUKA'S FACE?! YOU'RE NOT HIM!!
!
GIVE HIM BACK TO ME!
GRAB
STOP IT, MISAKI!
RITSUKA'S SICK!
I'M BEGGING YOU!! GIVE HIM BACK!
GET OUT OF HERE!
IT'S OKAY.
IF SHE WANTS TO BITE ME, SHE CAN BITE ME.
STING
I'm bleeding.
She'll break a tooth.
SHE CAN HIT ME AND CURSE AT ME.
AFTER ALL...

THIS IS A SIN FOR WHICH I DESERVE TO BE PUNISHED.

BING
BONG
SO...
TODAY...
AFTER YOU DRAW A PICTURE OF A FRIEND...
...WE'LL ALL TALK ABOUT FRIENDSHIP.
MURMUR
MURMUR
RITSUKA!
N4-479=79064-0
95 ¥1600E
there can be a misunderstanding relate
obliterate
R-RITSUKA.
WHAT ARE YOU READING?
HMM?
GRRRR

星空
星空
星空
星空

SORRY ABOUT THE OTHER DAY!
YUIKO WILL BE MORE THOUGHTFUL FROM NOW ON, SO CAN YOU FORGIVE HER?
RITSUKA?
Leave...
...me alone.
BOB
BOB
BOB
SORRY! SORRY!
PLEASE FORGIVE YUIKO!!

Papers: Starry Sky; student name

THEN YOU FORGIVE YUIKO?!
UH...
No...
I'm the one apologizing.
...
SURE.
Do you listen at all?
Oh, forget it.
HEH HEH.
HEH HEH...
HEH HEH HEH ...
She's so weird.
SO WHAT ARE YOU READING?
AN INTRO TO NIETZSCHE.
HUH?
HE TALKED ABOUT HOW "GOD IS DEAD." AND HE DIED OF VENEREAL DISEASE.
...SO IT'S INTERESTING?
YEAH, DO YOU WANT TO BORROW IT?
YUIKO DOESN'T READ.
She's illiterate ?!
BUT Y'KNOW ...
Tee hee!
YUIKO'S ASKING BECAUSE YUIKO WANTS TO KNOW!
...
THAT'S OKAY, ISN'T IT?
YEAH, THAT'S GOOD.
I DON'T LIKE PEOPLE WHO JUST BLINDLY OBEY.

OKAY!
EVERY-ONE FIND A BUDDY.
WHO-EVER YOU LIKE.
CHATTER
CHATTER
HUH?
HUH?
EH?
HUH?
WHAT ABOUT YUIKO?
WE'RE ALREADY PAIRED OFF.
DEAL WITH IT.
IDIOT.

YOU ALREADY HAVE SOMEBODY ELSE TO PAIR WITH, YUIKO.
RIGHT.
RIGHT.
RIGHT.
HUH?
EH?
REALLY?
HUH?
YUIKO'S THE ODD ONE OUT?
Oh boy.
What a cliché.
Exiled from the girls.

HEY!
Sigh. Man...
WHO'S GONNA DRAW FIRST?
RITSUKA ...
?
LOOK!
I'M SAYING I'LL PAIR UP WITH YOU.
You awake?
SCOOT
OH!
THANKS!
SHA
SHA
I can't watch.
DON'T GET IN-VOLVED WITH ME.
THEY'LL JUST LEAVE YOU OUT AGAIN.
HUH?
BUT YOU'RE ALWAYS SUPPOSED TO BE NICE TO A NEW STUDENT.
SHA
It's too dumb.

THAT'S WHAT YUIKO THINKS ANYWAY.
...
WELL, LOOK.
YOU'RE NOT A COMPLETE IDIOT AFTER ALL.
IT'S NOT "LOOK"! IT'S YUIKO!!
HMPH!
NO WAY.
SAY YUIKO!
HOW COME?!
WHAT'S WITH- OH.
WOW, RITSUKA. YOU SUCK AT ART.
WAH
WAH!
HEY!
DON'T LOOK!
BLUSH
YOU TWO! QUIET DOWN, PLEASE!
MRRRGH...
BEAM
BEAM
BEAM
MS. SHINONOME, HOW IS YOUR NEW STUDENT DOING?

QUITE WELL, THANKS!
HE SEEMS TO BE ADJUSTING.
NO BEHAVIOR PROBLEMS?
WHAT ...?
OF COURSE NOT.
HE'S A LITTLE SHORT WITH PEOPLE, BUT ASIDE FROM THAT...
IT'S JUST THAT HE'S BEEN THROUGH SOMETHING AWFUL, SO...
SAY...
...WHAT?
PEEK
YOU DIDN'T HEAR ABOUT THE INCIDENT? RITSUKA AOYAGI'S OLDER BROTHER WAS KILLED.
WHAT... RITSUKA'S BROTHER?
...!
Jonan Elementary School

Don't follow me.
No, Yuiko wants to walk home together!
Let's hang out!
You don't have cram school, right?
Let's play!
SOUBI ...!!
RITSUKA.
I MISSED YOU.
RITSUKA !
...
...
I WAS GOING TO GIVE THIS TO YOU THE NEXT TIME WE MET.
Not that ... again.
WHOA.
It's an adult!
WOW !
WHOA ...
SHUFF

HERE.
All 50.
OH... THE PHOTOS.
YOU PRINTED THEM OUT. THANKS.
THAT'S VERY NICE.
I'LL CHERISH THEM.
RITSUKA? WHO'S HE?
...
WHO'S THIS GUY?
HEY HEY!
THIS IS A PROBLEM.
TODAY...
LIKE BEFORE...
...RITSUKA HAS THAT DANGEROUS LOOK ON HIS FACE.
IT'S GOT NOTHING TO DO WITH YOU.
HEY, NO FAIR!
WHAT IS IT THAT YOU'RE SEARCHING FOR?
IF YOU DON'T LEARN TO CONCEAL THAT LOOK...
...THAT UNDISGUISED YEARNING...
...SOMEONE WILL SURELY STEAL YOU AWAY.

ARE YOU...
...BUSY NOW?
NEVER TOO BUSY FOR YOU.
THEN COME WITH ME.
I WANT YOU TO EXPLAIN WHAT ALL THAT STUFF YESTERDAY WAS ABOUT.
R...
RITSUKA !!
WHAT THE HECK ?!
You...
...startled me.
PLEASE!
DON'T LEAVE YUIKO OUT!
LET'S ALL GO TO YUIKO'S HOUSE! NO-BODY'S HOME.
Whoa.
FOOMP
YUIKO'S A LATCHKEY KID!
THEN SHALL WE...
...ALL GO?
LET'S GO! LET'S GO!
RITSUKA !
OKAY! ALL RIGHT!

OHH!
A CONVENIENCE STORE!
7 ELEVEn
コンビニエンス
銀行ATM
LET'S GO IN!
THERE'S NOTHING TO EAT AT HOME.
SURE.
HOLD ON A MINUTE!
YOU'RE NOT GOING TO EAT CONVENIENCE STORE FOOD, ARE YOU?
BUT YUIKO LIKES THEIR BURRITOS.
I LIKE IT TOO.
THAT'S NO GOOD ...
...FOR GROWING BODIES.
HOW COME?
WHAT DO YOU MEAN NO GOOD ...?
Tastes good.
AND CHEESECAKE AND PUDDING.
RICE BALLS AND BENTO LUNCHES.
I'LL MAKE SOMETHING WITH WHATEVER YOU HAVE AT YOUR HOUSE, YUIKO.

YUIKO'S NOT SUPPOSED TO USE THE KITCHEN WHEN YUIKO'S HOME ALONE.
OR TURN THE GAS ON AND STUFF.
WELL THEN...
WE JUST HAVE TO MAKE SURE WE DON'T LEAVE ANY EVIDENCE.
WHAT ?!
DON'T TEACH HER TO BE BAD!
YOU'RE AWFULLY PICKY.
BEFORE YOU FUSS ABOUT THE KITCHEN...
HMM... WHAT HAVE WE HERE? BURDOCK AND CHICKEN...
TUNK
WHO IS HE ?
UH, HE'S SOUBI...
I'M SOUBI AGATSUMA.
IT'S BAD?
YOU'RE SUPPOSED TO BE AN ADULT!
...MAYBE YOU SHOULDN'T LET STRANGERS IN THE HOUSE?
NO WAY I'M EATING BURDOCK, OKAY?
WHAT DO YOU LIKE, THEN?

MCDON-ALD'S.
UGH...
THAT'S FINE... EVERY NOW AND THEN.
YOU HAVE TO EAT RIGHT.
YOU NEED TO TRAIN ALL FIVE SENSES.
I'm borrowing this apron.
WHAT FIVE SENSES?
SIGHT, HEARING, SMELL, TOUCH AND TASTE.
WHY THE FIVE SENSES?
PEOPLE USUALLY JUST SAY JUNK FOOD'S BAD FOR YOUR HEALTH.
THE FIVE SENSES...
...RELY ON ORGANS THAT CAN BE TRAINED TO BE SENSI-TIVE.
FIRST YOU NEED TO TRAIN THE SENSORY ORGANS.
EYES, EARS, NOSE, SKIN, AND TONGUE.
EATING STIMULATES YOUR TASTE BUDS OF COURSE, AS WELL AS YOUR NOSE AND THE NERVE END-INGS IN YOUR TONGUE.
AND THE TONGUE IS VERY SENSITIVE, WHICH IS WHY IT HURTS WHEN BITTEN.

WHO'S GONNA BITE A TONGUE? NOT ME.
THAT'S GROSS.
YOU THINK SO?
IF YOU ASK ME, I'D SAY IT FEELS NICE.
HUH?!
SHFF
HERE WE GO.
CHICKEN AND SHAVED BURDOCK SPAGHETTI.
SMELLS AWE-SOME!
AND IT LOOKS DELI-CIOUS.
KAW
RITSUKA!
SOUBI!
SEE YOU TO-MOR-ROW!!
Ugh.
Again... ...tomor-row?
WAVE
KAW
ARE YOU COLD?
NOPE.
I'LL WALK YOU HOME.

SO ARE YOU...
...GOING TO EXPLAIN ABOUT THE OTHER DAY?
THE ONLY ONE WHO CAN FIGHT AGAINST THE ONES WHO KILLED SEIMEI...
...IS ME.
YOU WANT TO KILL THE ENEMY, RIGHT?
I LOVE YOU, RITSUKA.

I KNEW IN MY GUT...
HOW CAN HE TALK ABOUT MURDER...
...AND LOVE...
...IN THE SAME BREATH?
SO YOU KNOW?
YOU KNOW WHO KILLED SEIMEI?!
WHAT DO YOU KNOW?
WHO DID IT ...?
DID YOU LOOK FOR SEIMEI'S WILL?
... HE WASN'T LYING.
HIS WILL?
I NEVER THOUGHT ...
WHERE WOULD HIS WILL BE?!
I DIDN'T KNOW ADULTS COULD BE LIKE THIS.
HE'S SO STRANGE!
ONLY A SPELL BATTLE, FOUGHT WITH WORDS, WILL WORK AGAINST THIS ENEMY.
WE FIGHT IN PAIRS. I AM THE FIGHTER.

YOU ARE THE SACRIFICE, RITSUKA.
DURING BATTLE, THE SACRIFICE BEARS THE DAMAGE INFLICTED UPON THE FIGHTER.
IF THE SACRIFICE GETS WORN DOWN, YOU LOSE.
"SACRIFICE"? LIKE AN OFFERING!
BDMP
BDMP
IT IS VERY...
...VERY PAINFUL.
YOU WILL SUFFER. CAN YOU HANDLE IT?
BDMP
OF COURSE.
CAN YOU HANDLE UNBEARABLE SUFFERING, RITSUKA?
BDMP
I CAN DO IT!

SEIMEI'S WILL.
WHERE COULD IT BE ?
RITSUKA.
TMP TMP
WHAT IS IT?
I MADE YOUR FAVORITE DISHES.
YOU LIKE CHESTNUT RICE, DON'T YOU?
BAM BAM BAM
PLEASE COME OUT.
WHAT'S THE MATTER, RITSUKA ?
BAM BAM
IT'S JUST... I'M SORRY, MOM.
LATER.
BAM
JUST WAIT.
BAM BAM
NO.
GET OUT HERE, RITSUKA!
RITSUKA !
BAM BAM
THE COMPUTER !!
RITSUKA!
IT'S OKAY, MOM.
I'LL BE THERE SOON.
BAM BAM BAM BAM
I HAVEN'T TURNED IT ON SINCE SEIMEI DIED.
ZWEE—E

TAK
TAK
HUH?
GOOD EVENING.
...
THIS IS THE SECOND FLOOR.
CHAK
AND? I'M HERE.
BAM
SHE'S MAKING A FUSS. SHALL I SILENCE HER?
THAT'S MY MOTHER.
WHATEVER YOU WANT. I'LL DO WHATEVER YOU LIKE.
BAM
SHE'S MY MOTHER AND SEIMEI'S TOO. DON'T DO ANY-THING.
JUST LEAVE HER ALONE.
TAK
IS THIS IT?
ARGH ...
TAK
TAK
RITSUKA
THE ENTIRE FOLDER IS LOCKED.
WHAT'S THE PASSWORD ?

PLEASE ENTER YOUR ID AND PASSWORD.
ID:
RITSUKA
PASSWORD:
PASS-WORD...
...
MAYBE "BELOVED"...?
TAK
TAK
DAMN.
BWOOP
INPUT FAILED. TRY AGAIN?
CANCEL
THAT'S NOT IT.
HOW ABOUT...
HEY...
GULP
WHAT DID YOU CALL ME?
YOUR REAL NAME, RITSUKA, IS...
LOVELESS.
英数
IT MEANS "WITHOUT LOVE."
THAT'S HORRIBLE...
WHAT'S THE DEAL WITH THAT?
WHO DECIDED THAT?!

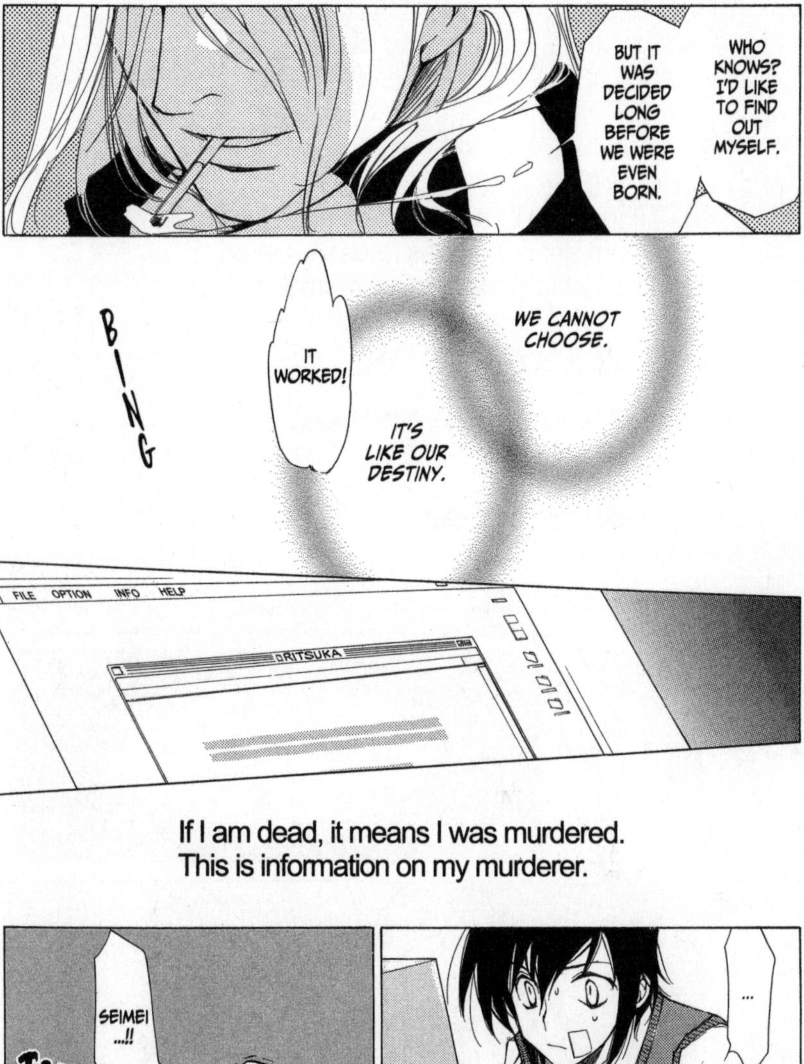

WHO KNOWS? I'D LIKE TO FIND OUT MYSELF.

BUT IT WAS DECIDED LONG BEFORE WE WERE EVEN BORN.

WE CANNOT CHOOSE.

IT'S LIKE OUR DESTINY.

IT WORKED!

BING

FILE OPTION INFO HELP

RITSUKA

If I am dead, it means I was murdered.
This is information on my murderer.

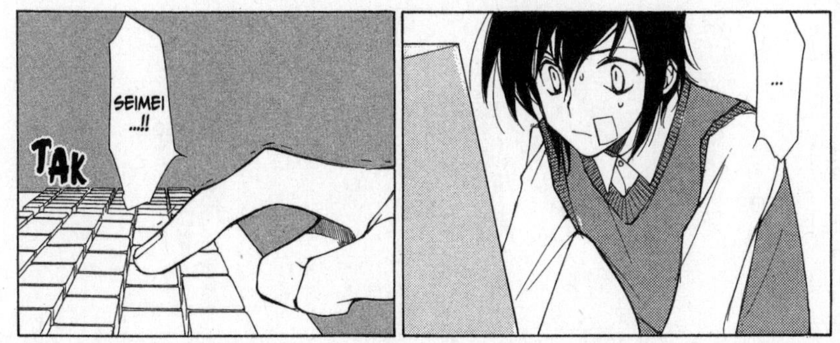

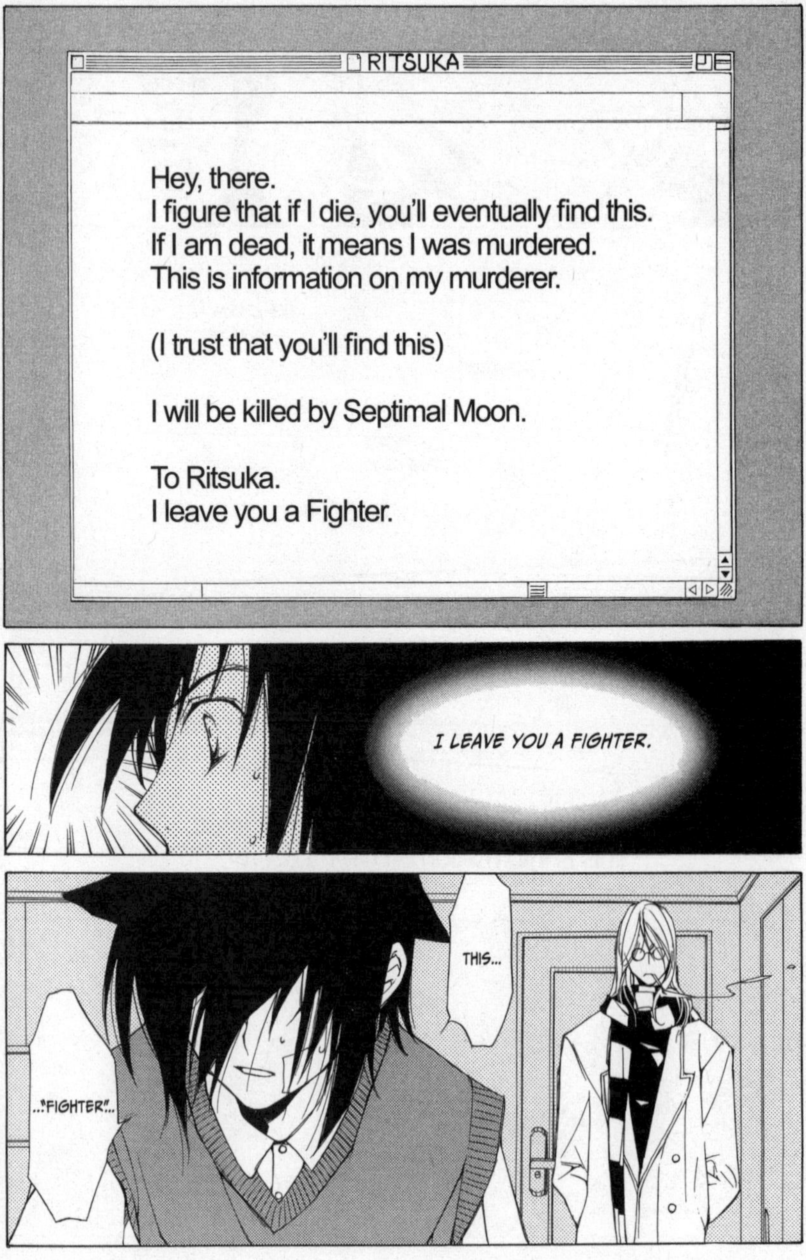

RITSUKA

Hey, there.
I figure that if I die, you'll eventually find this.
If I am dead, it means I was murdered.
This is information on my murderer.

(I trust that you'll find this)

I will be killed by Septimal Moon.

To Ritsuka.
I leave you a Fighter.

I LEAVE YOU A FIGHTER.

THIS...
..."FIGHTER"...

WHAT IS THE MEANIN OF THIS SOUBI
WHAT IS THIS?!
FWIP
YOU'RE HERE BECAUSE SEIMEI TOLD YOU TO FIND ME?
THAT'S RIGHT.
YOU SAID...
YOU SAID YOU LOVED ME!!
OVER AND OVER!
WHY?
JUST BECAUSE SEIMEI TOLD YOU TO?!
RITSUKA'S VOICE IS ELECTRIFYING.
ANSWER ME!
SOUBI!!
IT'S THE VOICE...
...OF THE ONE WHO WILL COMMAND ME.

YES.

DID SEIMEI ...

...TELL YOU TO LOVE ME?

HE DID.

SO YOU JUST DO WHATEVER SEIMEI SAYS.

YOU'RE FINE WITH THAT?

I AM.

SEIMEI'S WORD IS ABSOLUTE.

AND NOW I'VE BEEN TOLD TO OBEY RITSUKA'S COMMANDS.

YOU CAN'T LOVE SOMEONE...

...BECAUSE YOU WERE COMMANDED TO.

THAT'S NOT RIGHT...!!

BUT I LOVE YOU.
SHUT UP!
I DON'T WANT TO HEAR IT!!

BUT YOU'RE STILL GOING TO NEED ME.
ONLY I CAN FIGHT FOR YOU.
THERE'S NO USE CRYING ABOUT IT.
I'M NOT...
...CRYING !!
THERE'S NOTHING!!
THERE'S NOTHING THAT BELONGS TO ME!
NOT SEIMEI OR SOUBI OR MOM!
NOTHING...!

I'LL NEVER FORGIVE WHOEVER KILLED SEIMEI. WHAT DID SEIMEI EVER DO TO DESERVE SOMETHING LIKE THAT?!

CHIRP

MURMUR

MURMUR

IT'S TRUE, I SWEAR!

I HEARD THE TEACHERS TALKING ABOUT IT.

SEE HERE?

THE VICTIM WAS SEIMEI AOYAGI, AGE 17.

MURMUR

THE SHOCKED CLASSROOM!!

THAT'S AOYAGI'S OLDER BROTHER.

"HE WAS SET ON FIRE WHILE STILL ALIVE."

"AND AFTERWARDS, THE BODY WAS RE-CLOTHED AND LEFT IN AN ELEMENTARY SCHOOL CLASSROOM."

"THE CULPRIT HAS NOT YET BEEN FOUND."

FREAKY!

I'M PRETTY CURIOUS MYSELF, YOU KNOW.
ABOUT WHO KILLED MY BROTHER.
I'M GOING TO KILL THEM TOO.
YOU KNOW ...
...THEY LEFT HIM IN MY SEAT.
GASP
MY BROTHER'S CORPSE.
IF YOU GET TOO CLOSE TO ME...
...YOU MIGHT GET KILLED, BURNED AND LEFT IN MY CHAIR TOO.
!!
EW, GROSS !!
WAAAAH

TMP
TMP
TMP
RITSUKA!
TMP
TMP
RITSUKA! UH...
YUIKO'S REALLY SORRY!
WAIT!
LOOK, SHUT UP! DON'T APOLOGIZE.
IT'S NOT YOUR BUSINESS!
GRAB
LET GO!
BUT... YUIKO FEELS BAD!
LET HER MAKE IT UP TO YOU!
TUG
DON'T BOTHER ME! LET GO!
NO!
NO...
NO...
YUIKO...
SOB...
...WANTS TO BE...
...FRIENDS WITH YOU, RITSUKA...
I'M...
JUST...
WHATEVER. I DON'T NEED ANYBODY.
I'M TIRED.

IT DOESN'T MATTER IF I LAUGH OR CRY ANYMORE.

SO WHY SMILE?

IT JUST WEARS ME OUT!

SORRY RITSUKA. YUIKO DOESN'T GET IT...

BUT... YOU SOUND LONELY.

HUG

YUIKO HATES BEING LONELY!!

YUIKO DOESN'T WANT YOU TO BE LONELY, RITSUKA!

YUIKO'S HERE FOR YOU!

NGH...

YUIKO'S HERE FOR YOU.

YUIKO WILL BE YOUR FRIEND... SO PLEASE!!

DON'T CRY.

YO!
LOVE-LESS.
FLINCH
WHERE'S SOUBI? HE'S NOT HERE?
YOU ...!
...
HUH? WHAT HOME-ROOM ARE THEY FROM?
WE'RE HERE TO COLLECT YOU.
BY ORDER OF SEPTIMAL MOON.
GASP

SEPTIMAL MOON...?
YOU TWO!

WHAT...
WHAT'S GOING ON?
GO BACK TO THE CLASS-ROOM.
CALL SOUBI.
YOU AREN'T GONNA COME QUIETLY, ARE YOU?
BUT... RITSUKA?
IT'S FINE, JUST HURRY.
GO BACK.
BUT...
YUIKO!
I'LL MAKE IT UP TO YOU LATER, SO JUST DO IT.
BLUSH
I JUST WANT TO ASK ONE THING.
WHY DID YOU KILL SEIMEI?
TMP TMP
NO COM-MENT.

CHAPTER 3

C'MON.
YOU'RE COMING BACK WITH US.
AS IF I'D EVER GO WITH THEM!
ABOUT SEIMEI... WHY DID YOU KILL HIM?
GLANCE
GRR!
!
HMPH
NO COM-MENT.

YOU DIDN'T DENY IT.
YOU REALLY... MURDERED HIM?
IT'S NOT LIKE I DID IT PERSON-ALLY.
SEPTIMAL MOON KILLED HIM.
WHAT IS SEPTIMAL MOON?
NO COM-MENT!
WHY ARE YOU HARASSING ME?
NO COM-MENT!
C'MON, IT DOESN'T MATTER. JUST DO AS YOU'RE TOLD!
PLEASE. LIKE I'M GOING TO LISTEN TO YOU.
FEH
WHY BOTHER ASKING?
FIGURES.
BUT IT'S ALREADY BEEN DECIDED THAT YOU'RE COMING TO SEPTIMAL MOON.
WHAT YOU WANT HAS NOTHING TO DO WITH IT.
NOK NOK

DID I KEEP YOU WAITING...
RITSUKA?
BLUSH
SOUBI.
WHAT DO I DO...?
YOU SAID THAT YOU'D FIGHT FOR ME, RIGHT?
OF COURSE. WE'LL FIGHT.
CLAK
CLAK
JUST TRUST ME.
I WANT TO BELIEVE HIM.

LET US BATTLE.
VWEEN
AGREED!!
VWEEN

SYSTEMS EXPAND.
OVER AND OVER!!
DESTROY!!
DOOH
DEFEND!!
DEFEND!!
THAT WITHOUT SHAPE SHALL PROTECT THIS BODY.
BWOOO
NO POWER CAN REACH ME.
SHAA

RE-VERSE!
RE-FLECT!
RE-PULSE!
POWER DIS-CHARGED...
...SHALL RETURN TO THE SOURCE.
!!
HE'S FAST!
VIP
AGH!
HE DEFLECT-ED IT!
VIP
DEFEND!
DEFEND!!
DEFEND!!
VIP
VIP
CALM DOWN, AI.
THAT WON'T WORK.
JUST REPEATING THE SAME WORD IS INEFFECTIVE.
MI-DORI!
DO YOU EVEN KNOW WHAT YOU'RE DOING?

RIP!!
BLAST!!
FWOOO
SHWAAAA
PSHA
PSHA
PSHA
!!!
CHANG
AGH!!
WH...
WHAT'S THAT?
THAT'S A RESTRICTION.
RESTRICTION
IT'S THE DAMAGE THAT A SACRIFICE RECEIVES.

MIDORI!
THIS IS NOTHING! KEEP GOING!
IT'S MORE IMPORTANT FOR YOU TO REACT PROPERLY.
HE'S CHOOSING HIS WORDS QUICKLY AND PRECISELY.
AND HE'S LINKING THEM TOGETHER.
YOU WON'T BE ABLE TO ATTACK IF YOU'RE BUSY DEFENDING ME.
IF YOU RESTRICT THAT SACRIFICE...
...YOU CAN INFLICT FOUR TIMES THE NORMAL AMOUNT OF DAMAGE.
FWOOO
AFTER ALL, THEIR NAMES ARE DIFFERENT.
TRY CUTTING.
GOT IT.
C..
CUT APART.
SEVER.
OOO
KREEEE
ROTATE.
DIF-FRACT.
DIVERT THE BODY'S COURSE OF ORBIT!
CUT APART THE BODY.
WHETHER A LITTLE SLICE OR A BIG GASH...
FWOOO
I'LL CUT THEM APART!
CUTTING (OF

BZZRT
NGH...
SHANK
CHANG
I DID IT!
!!
CHANG
CUT AGAIN!
CUT APART!
FWOOVWEEEE
THAT ATTACK IS FUTILE. EVADE AND RECUPERATE.
ONCE MORE, ROTATE AND DIFFRACT.
INSCRIBE AN ORBIT.
NGH...
CHANG
I DIDN'T DODGE WELL ENOUGH?

HUFF ...
AH ...
It's tight.
DOES IT HURT, RITSUKA ?
THIS ...
GASP
DID SEIMEI... DO THIS TOO?
THAT'S RIGHT.
YOU'RE SO BRAVE.
OW.
THEN I CAN HANDLE IT!
CLINK
CUT...
DENY !!
NGH!

STOP.
SUS-PEND.
INTER-FERE.
INTER-VENE.
I SHALL INFLUENCE AND INVADE YOU.
I SHALL INFILTRATE AND IMPEDE YOUR ESCAPE. I SHALL SWALLOW YOUR FREEDOM AND LOCK YOU DOWN.
NGH ...
DEFEND!
FULL POWER ...!!
BSH
BSH
AGH!!
FAIL.
DEFENSE FAILS.
FWOOO
ALL WALLS WILL CRUMBLE.
CLANK
RITSUKA.
KISS ME.

HUH ...
WHAT ?!
CHANG
WHA ...?!
WHOA!
NO WAY !!
NGH ...
ZSH
FALL TO CHAOS ...
LITTLE BRATS WITH YOUR LITTLE EARS!
I KNOW THINGS THAT YOU DON'T KNOW.
DEFEAT
ANNIHILATE !!

...

RIT-SUKA?
YOU OKAY?
JOLT

THOSE GUYS ARE SEPTIMAL MOON!
WHAT ARE YOU GOING TO DO WITH THEM ...?

YOU SAID *YOU* WERE GOING TO KILL THEM.
BUT IT'S FINE. I'LL DO WHATEVER YOU LIKE.

WHAT DO YOU WANT ME TO DO?
KILL THEM?

...!!
GULP

...
NO...
I'M NOT GOING TO KILL PEOPLE.
GRIT

I WON'T KILL...!
THEN I'M GOING TO GO RETURN THEM.
THERE'S A GOOD BOY.
I LOVE YOU ... RITSUKA.
I DON'T...
I DON'T WANT TO HEAR IT!!
JUST GO AWAY !!
SKWEE
SEE YOU.
HOW CAN YOU SAY "I LOVE YOU" ...?

I HEAR THOSE WORDS AND YOU KISS ME...
SOUBI.
...AND I START TO BELIEVE YOU.
NGH...
I've had... enough!
NGH...
WHAT AM I SUPPOSED TO DO?
WHY ARE YOU...?
WHY DID YOU HAVE TO COME HERE AND TURN ME ALL UPSIDE DOWN?

I'LL KEEP MY PROMISE.
DO YOU STILL WANT TO BE FRIENDS?
My head hurts.
REALLY?! YUIKO CAN?!

IT'S "I."
TRY IT.
OKAY!
I.
I!!

THAT'S IT.
I LIKE IT... THAT'S BETTER.
YUIKO LIKES... I MEAN, I...
BLUSH
I LOVE RITSUKA'S SMILE.
And also, you need to get smarter.
I hate idiots.
Like you.
Whaaaat?
Read more books! Read! I thought you were illiterate!
Got it! So I need to read, right?
Exactly.
I LOVE IT SO MUCH.
HAWATARI... LET'S GO.
OKAY!!

I DON'T THINK ANYONE IN CLASS HAS EVER DONE THIS.
Erk!!
HOW DOES THAT MAKE YOU FEEL?
DON'T YOU FEEL CLEVER?
OR...
...
DO YOU FEEL DIRTY?

...
YOU'RE...
...SURPRISINGLY CHILDISH.

Hmph!
Idiot.

BELOVED

BELOVED

YUN KOUGA

WHAT DO YOU WANT ME TO DO?
CHAPTER 4

RITSUKA.SOUBI+SEIMEI
LOVELESS..........NO_00

PING! ♡

RITSUKA AOYAGI?
WHO'S THAT?
HE SHOWED UP WHILE YOU WERE OUT, YAYOI.
HE'S A TRANSFER STUDENT.
NOD
NOD
...
A TRANSFER STUDENT ...
I'M NOT INTER-ESTED.
BUT THIS GUY...
TO YUIKO...?!
...IS REALLY CLOSE TO HAWATARI.
WHAT?

HOW...
...IS THAT...
RITSUKA!!
FWIP!!
YU...
GOOD MORNING!
WOW! ♡
YOU ALWAYS LOOK SO COOL.
"COOL"...!
MORNING, YUIKO.
Man, you're loud.
YOU READ THAT BOOK I TOLD YOU ABOUT YESTER-DAY?
UH HUH!
I SURE DID!
HE'S ACTING SO FRIENDLY WITH HER.
?!?

BUT...
HE'S A...
HE'S TOTALLY SHORT!!
...SHRIMP!
Y...
YAYOI?
BDMP
Shrimp?
Me?
Is that me?
HMPH
KRNCH
WELL, EXCUSE ME FOR BEING SHORT.
BUT...

YOU'RE A SHRIMP YOURSELF.
SHOCK
MY HEIGHT IS IRRELEVANT.
THE ISSUE HERE IS THAT *YOU'RE* SHORT.
KACHING
Two times?
He said it twice?!
WHAT'S IT TO YOU WHETHER I'M SHORT OR MY TAIL'S LONG OR IF MY EARS ARE COOL-LOOKING?
I DON'T GET WHAT YOUR PROBLEM IS.

THE ONLY PEOPLE WHO HAVE PERMISSION TO DATE HER...
AAUGH!
...ARE GUYS WHO ARE TALLER THAN SHE IS!
SHORT PEOPLE AREN'T QUALIFIED!
TO GO OUT WITH YUIKO!
WAIT! WAIT!
YAYOI!
HUH?!
WHO CARES ABOUT THAT?
BLUNT
...
...
UH-HUH.
SHRUG
...
IT'S NOT LIKE WE'RE DATING.
WE'RE JUST FRIENDS.
RIGHT, YUIKO?
!!
!!
!!

YUIKO ...!!
YOU'RE...
FWOO
YUIKO.
WILL YOU GO OUT WITH ME?
UH...
YAYOI ?!
BLUSH
WITH YUIKO?!
NO...
NO WAY! NO WAY! NO WAY!
YUIKO CAN'T!!
PANIC
NO!
SHAKE
WHOA!
YUIKO!
CALM DOWN!

BLUSH
UH...
IS IT...
...BECAUSE YOU DON'T LIKE ME...?
FIVE TIMES...
SHE SAID NO FIVE TIMES...
SNIFF...
YUIKO LIKES YOU, YAYOI. WE'RE FRIENDS AND STUFF...
BUT YUIKO'S ONLY IN SIXTH GRADE.

ONLY IN SIXTH GRADE...? MIDDLE SCHOOLERS DATE!
MONDA'S BEEN DATING SINCE FOURTH GRADE. SUZUKI TOO...
D-DID I JUMP THE GUN...?
SHOCK
UH... UM... OKAY?
WAAAH
SORRY!

SORRY!
YAYOI...
ACK...
OH NO, I MADE HER CRY!
IT'S OKAY, YUIKO.
I'M THE ONE WHO SHOULD BE APOLOGIZING.
SHOCK

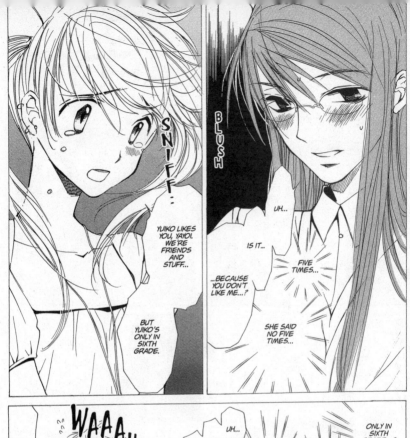

CRACK
YUIKO CAN'T GO OUT WITH PEOPLE WHO'RE SHORTER THAN HER.
168cm
Thanks.
147 cm
THAT...
I...
WHA...
OH...
WHAT'S...
TRMBL
UNGH...
TRMBL
I SEE NOW...
YES! THAT'S IT.
SORRY.
BWAAAAH
I'M THE ONE...
TRMBL
...WHO WANTS TO CRY.
TRMBL
TRMBL
!!
WE'RE GOING TO BE LATE.
LET'S GO, YUIKO.

SEE THAT?
HOW IS *THAT* NOT DATING?!
THAT'S WHAT AOYAGI SAYS...
...CONTRARY TO THE EVIDENCE.
WHO THE HELL WAS THAT GUY? HE WAS WEIRD...
I...
I'M SORRY, RITSUKA.
WHY ARE YOU APOLOGIZING, YUIKO?
SOR...
BESIDES, HEIGHT DOESN'T MATTER. THAT'S STUPID.
SOR...
~~Yuiko~~ I mean, I...
WHO DOES THAT YAYOI THINK HE IS?
STRUT
HE'S GOT A GIRLY NAME.
STRUT

RITSUKA AOYAGI. SIXTH GRADE, CLASS 3.
HE'S CUTE, ISN'T HE?
LIKE A GIRL.
ANYWAY, I FIGURE I'M GOING TO GROW SOON...
...AND GET A LOT TALLER.
AFTER ALL, SEIMEI WAS TALL.

OKAY.
I'M HANDING BACK YOUR MATH TESTS.
THE TOP SCORE WAS 100! RITSUKA AOYAGI!!
BUT EVERYONE DID PRETTY WELL THIS TIME.
I'M REALLY PROUD OF YOU! ♡
YAY
ANDO!
ITO!
Here!
UDA-GAWA!
YAY
RITSUKA, THAT'S GREAT! ♡
YOU GOT A PERFECT SCORE! ♡
WELL, THERE'S ONLY ONE POSSIBLE ANSWER IN MATH.
YOU SHOULD GET A PERFECT SCORE TOO, YUIKO.
Make Ms. Shinonome happy.

THAT'S IMPOSSIBLE.
NO WAY.
WHAAAA?!
DON'T SAY THINGS ARE IMPOSSIBLE.
I HATE THAT WORD.
DON'T TALK LIKE THAT.
DUMMY.
OKAY, THAT'S ALL FOR TODAY.
CLEANING TIME!
BING BONG
ATTENTION!
SKRUT
SKRUT
SKRU
TOMORROW IS SATURDAY, BUT IT'S PARENTS' DAY.
ENCOURAGE YOUR FATHER TO COME!
OKAY!
BOW!
GOODBYE!
CHATTER
CHATTER
Library time?
Yeah.
RITSUKA.
CAN I HAVE A WORD WITH YOU?

...

YES.

YUIKO, GO AHEAD TO THE LIBRARY.

HUUUUH?

YOU SEE...

RITSUKA, IT'S JUST...

THERE HASN'T BEEN A SIGNATURE SHOWING THAT YOUR PARENTS HAVE SEEN YOUR SCHOOL-WORK. THE "I'VE READ IT" CONFIRMATION?

SO I WAS WONDERING WHAT WAS GOING ON...?

Oh...

That...

SOUBI...
...IS HERE!!
I WANT TO SEE HIM...
AFTER ALL, EVEN IF I SEE HIM...
I DON'T WANT TO SEE HIM...
SOUBI'S HERE TO PICK YOU UP.
I'M GONNA WAIT WITH HIM!
TMP TMP
HEY...
YUIKO.
HE ISN'T HERE TO PICK US UP.
HE JUST CAME BECAUSE HE FELT LIKE IT...

BECAUSE HE FELT LIKE IT...
SELFISH SOUBI...
IF I SEE HIM...
...HE'S JUST GOING TO MESS ME UP AGAIN.
I WANT TO SEE HIM...
...BUT...
...IT HURTS TO SEE HIM...

RITSUKA ?!
WHO'S THAT...?
OH.
HIM?
HIS NAME IS AGATSUMA.
HE WAS A FRIEND OF MY DEAD BROTHER.

AND, UH...
HE...
...HANGS OUT WITH ME SOME-TIMES.
I SEE...
OH...

LATER, I'VE GOTTA GO.
DASH
HEY.
RITSUKA, WAIT. YOU NEED TO GET THAT SIGNATURE.

SIGNA-TURE?
REALLY ?
I DON'T NEED IT, DO I? I GET GOOD GRADES.
MY PARENTS DON'T SAY ANYTHING ANYWAY.

THAT'S NOT WHAT I MEAN.
YOU NEED TO HAVE THEM SEE IT AND GET IT SIGNED.
THAT'S WEIRD.
FINE, THEN.
IF YOU WANT IT, THEN I'LL HAVE THEM DO IT.
I'll sign.
HEY NOW!
RITSUKA!!
THAT'S THE FIRST TIME I'VE SEEN...
...THAT EXPRESSION ON RITSUKA'S FACE.
HE LOOKED SO CUTE.
I WONDER WHO THIS AGATSUMA IS.

MY BROTHER SEIMEI...

HE ALWAYS TALKED TO ME...

...IN A WAY I COULD UNDERSTAND.

BUT SOUBI...

HE ALWAYS HAS SECRETS... HE'S ALWAYS HIDING THINGS... ALWAYS LYING...

RITSUKA! WHAT'S THE MATTER ?
I TOLD YOU TO RUN WHEN MOM STARTS GETTING OUT OF CONTROL, RIGHT?
QUITE THE BUMP YOU'VE GOT THERE.
I'M OKAY.
THIS IS NOTHING.
IT DOESN'T HURT.
JUST RUN.
IF MOM IS ABOUT TO DO SOME-THING TO YOU...
...JUST RUN TO ME.
PLCH
OKAY?
...
...
OKAY.
BUT NOW...

I HAVE NOWHERE TO RUN.
SOUBI!
HUFF
Jerk.
Jerk!!
DAMMIT...
YOU-!
HUFF
Jerk.
Jerk.
WHY ARE YOU HERE?!
WHAT THE HELL DO YOU WANT NOW?!
YOU'RE LATE!
HOW LONG DO YOU THINK IT'S BEEN?!
THREE DAYS, I THINK?
THAT'S RIGHT! YOU LEFT ME HANGING FOR THREE WHOLE DAYS!

YOU CAN JUST...!
WH ...?!
THAT'S NOT IT!!
Hmm.
YOU CAN JUST...
..."LOVE ME"?
TWITCH
YOU CAN JUST...
..."DIE"?
NO!
YOU JERK!
DON'T USE THAT WORD. I HATE IT.

RITSUKA! WHAT'S WRONG?
YOU'RE SCARING ME.
EEP!
Ngh!
!!
I...
I'm losing it.
UH...
NO, I...

SOUBI SAID HE WAS BUSY WITH HOME-WORK.
?
HOME-WORK...?
YES.
I'M A STUDENT.

A... STU-DENT?
He is?
I...
...didn't know.
YOU, SOUBI?

YES, I'M A COLLEGE STUDENT.
SORRY I COULDN'T COME SEE YOU.

WOW!
YOU'RE GOING OUT WITH A COLLEGE STUDENT, RITSUKA!
What?!
Do you hear yourself?
NO.
WE'RE NOT DATING.
WE'RE MASTER AND SERVANT.

MUSTARD...
AND ...?
What?
What's that...
...supposed to mean?
SPIN
SPIN

SHFF
I CAME HERE TO CONNECT WITH YOU.

HERE.

WHAT'S THIS ...?

MY NUMBER IS THE FIRST ONE IN THE ADDRESS BOOK.

CALL ME ANYTIME.

WHATEVER. I'M NOT DOING THAT.

AWW. HOW COME? JUST CALL ME.

HERE'S THE CHARGER.

YOU CAN ALSO SEND ME EMAIL.
YOU KNOW HOW, RIGHT?
HERE.

SKWEEZ
I CAN'T... ACCEPT THIS.
I DON'T KNOW WHY YOU'RE DOING THIS.

THERE'S A PERFECTLY GOOD REASON. IT'S SO YOU WON'T BE LONELY, RITSUKA.
SO YOU WON'T GET ANXIOUS.
YOU'LL ALWAYS BE CONNECTED TO ME.

Tel...
Telephone.
Phone.
I'M NOT LONELY.
Cell phone.
OH?
THAT'S GREAT, THEN!
PWEEP PWEEP PWEEP

HUH?
KIO?
...
YAY!
CAN I PUT MY NUMBER IN YOUR PHONE?

I'LL BE BACK SOON.
I'M A LITTLE BUSY RIGHT NOW.
YOU'RE NOT GONNA MAKE IT IN TIME.
IF YOU MISS THE DEADLINE THE PROFESSOR WON'T ACCEPT YOUR WORK.
YOU'RE FRIGGIN' *BUSY?*
ISN'T THAT RICH!
HURRY UP AND GET YOUR BUTT BACK HERE.
JEEZ.
AGATSUMA'S SURE GOT IT TOGETHER.
I'M BARELY COMING IN UNDER THE WIRE.
YOU CALL THIS "TOGETHER"?! HE HASN'T FINISHED ANY OF HIS WORK.
WHAT'S THIS "I'M BUSY" CRAP?

AND WHAT'S WITH THIS PICTURE?
IS HE SOME KIND OF PEDO?
FWIP
WOW, WHAT A CUTIE!

KIO.
DON'T GO THROUGH AGATSUMA'S BAG.
HE DOESN'T CARE!!
RUSTL
I'M PRETTY MUCH SOU'S WIFE, ANYWAY!!
I NEED TO CHECK!
UM...

OMIGOD, LOOK AT ALL OF THESE!
FWIP
THAT PERVERT!!
CHEATER!
EEE! HE'S SO CUTE.
AH HA, HE'S GOT HIS EARS!

I WON'T FORGIVE HIM FOR THIS!
NOT WHEN HE HAS SOMEONE LIKE ME!!
GRR
GRR
GRR
GRR
ARGH, I'M CALLING HIM.
AGH!
THAT PUNK.
HE TURNED HIS PHONE OFF.
DAMN IT. THAT BASTARD!
KIO.
COME ON BACK.

YOU'RE A COLLEGE STUDENT...
WHAT ARE YOU...
...STUDYING?
ART.
JAPANESE ART.
JAPANESE...
...ART...?
I FOUND OUT FOR THE FIRST TIME TODAY...
...?
THAT'S AMAZING.
ONE OF SOUBI'S SECRETS.

YOU THINK SO?
IT IS!! I CAN'T DRAW AT ALL.
RIGHT, YUIKO?!
BDMP
BDMP
BDMP
YUP!
TOTALLY AMAZING!!
BDMP

NEVER ONCE SINCE I MET HIM...
...HAVE I BELIEVED THAT HE REALLY WAS A HUMAN BEING...
...LIKE ME.
THEN NEXT TIME...
...I'LL PAINT A PICTURE FOR YOU, RITSUKA.
SOUBI.

HE GOES TO COLLEGE...
HE PAINTS PICTURES...
REALLY?
SURE.
YAY!
WOW WOW WOW WOW WOW
WHAT ARE YOU GOING TO PAINT?
MY SPECIALTY IS FLOWERS.
YOU FINALLY SMILED.
I'M GLAD TO SEE YOU'RE IN A BETTER MOOD NOW.

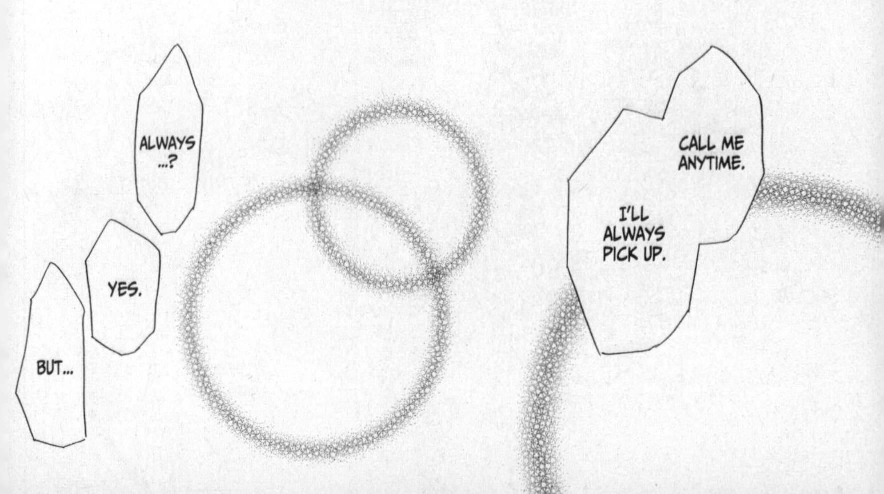

YOU CAN'T *ALWAYS* ANSWER THE PHONE. THAT'S IMPOSSIBLE.
I CAN.
IF IT'S A CALL FROM YOU, I'LL ALWAYS PICK UP.
DON'T PROMISE SOMETHING YOU CAN'T DO.
TRY ME.
I LIVE FOR YOU, RITSUKA.
THERE'S NOTHING I CAN'T DO.

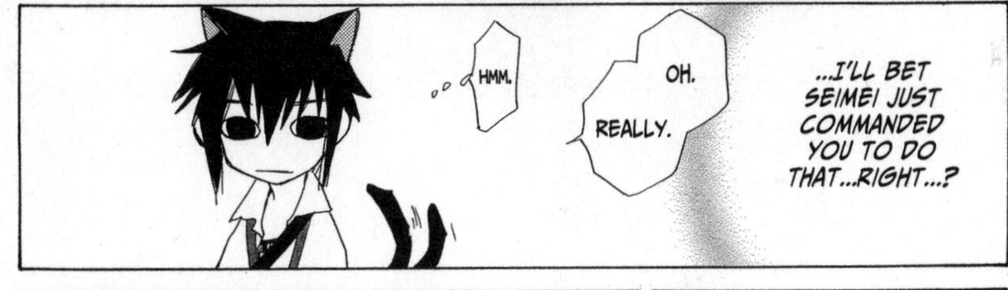

RITSUKA.
YOU'VE GOT SUCH SLENDER SHOULDERS.
IT'S ADORABLE.
BUT...
I'M SORRY.
NOW THE TRAINING BEGINS.
...

BRM
RM
WHAT'S WITH THIS LIBRARY CARD?
BOTH SIDES FILLED IN ONLY A WEEK?!
6-3
RITSUKA AOYAGI
DAY
TITLE
11/17 Bill Gates
11/17 Marsha and Dots
Disneyland
RITSUKA AOYAGI AGAIN?
YAYOI!
LET'S GO HOME.
WAIT A MINUTE.
I'M COMING...

HIS CALLI-GRAPHY ....
...IS REALLY GOOD TOO.

Paper: Sunset, Sixth grade Class 3, Ritsuka Aoyagi

AH. RITSUKA AND I HAVE THAT IN COMMON TOO.
SIGH...
?

I WONDER IF HE GOT THAT INJURY FROM GYM CLASS.
I GUESS THAT MEANS HE'S IN GOOD SHAPE...

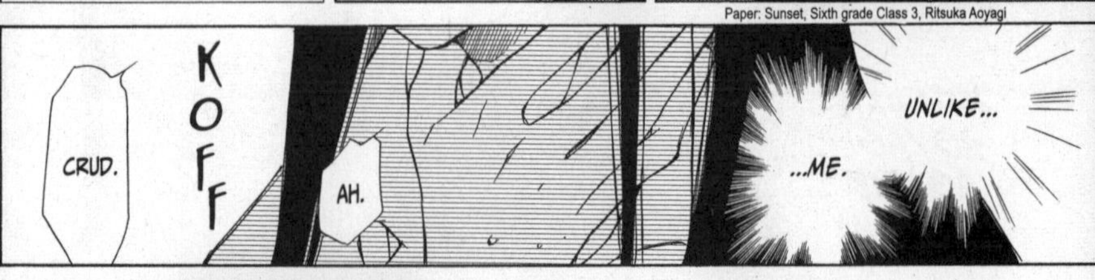

UNLIKE...
...ME.
AH.
KOFF
CRUD.

WSH
YAYOI !
YAYOI ...
YOU ALL RIGHT ?
KOFF !

YEAH.
I HAVE MY INHALER, SO I'M OKAY...
GASP
GASP
GASP
IT MUST BE THE LOW ATMO-SPHERIC PRESSURE ...

IT LOOKS LIKE IT'S ABOUT TO RAIN...
HURTS TO BREATHE.
GASP
GASP
...BUT...
I CAN'T ...
...GIVE UP ON YUIKO ...
...JUST BECAUSE OF HIM.
GASP
PLIP
PLIP
AW MAN.
IT'S REALLY COMING DOWN.
PLIP
THANK YOU VERY MUCH.
CHAK
OH.

GOT IT IN ON TIME, SOU?
SORT OF.
MY PAINTS HAVEN'T DRIED YET...
Ha ha.
THAT'S WHAT YOU GET FOR SKIPPING OUT, IDIOT.
AND?
CHK
"AND"?
WHO IS HE? THAT KID IN THE PICTURE. IT'S NOT OKAY!
LOOK, KIO.
DON'T GO POKING THROUGH PEOPLE'S BAGS...
GRR
GRRAR
SHUT UP! THAT'S NOT THE ISSUE HERE!
I ASKED YOU A QUESTION, SO ANSWER ME. WHO IS THAT KID?!
THAT BOY...
...IS RITSUKA AOYAGI.
THAT'S ALL I'LL SAY.
GRR
AOYAGI?!
WHAT?!

SLUMP
MY HEAD HURTS.
"AOYAGI" ?! THAT'S BAD!
AGH! IT COULDN'T GET ANY WORSE!
HE'S GOT SOMETHING TO DO WITH SEIMEI, RIGHT...?
PEEK
OH MY GOD... HIS KID?
DON'T BE ABSURD.
SEIMEI STILL HAD HIS EARS.
IT'S HIS LITTLE BROTHER.
Oops, I said it.
AGH!
MAN...
THIS SUCKS.
THIS REALLY, REALLY SUCKS.
SOU, YOU'RE GOING TO BECOME ANOTHER AOYAGI'S SLAVE?
JUST WHEN ...
...SEIMEI WAS FINALLY GONE.
KIO.
DON'T SAY THINGS LIKE THAT.
SHH

NOPE.
I'M SAYING IT.
I WAS THRILLED WHEN SEIMEI DIED.
KIO!!
HE SHACKLED YOU, SOU.
I DIDN'T MIND.
WELL, I DID! I'LL NEVER FORGIVE HIM.
LOOK, SOU, IF YOU'RE INTO THAT KIND OF THING...
...WHY CAN'T IT BE WITH ME?
I'LL BRUTALIZE YOU UNTIL YOU CAN'T STAND IT.
...
I'M NOT KINKY.
WHAT ?! YOU'RE LYING !!
KCHAK
HEY! STOP MAKING ALL THAT RACKET!
IF YOU'RE DONE CLEANING UP, THEN JUST GO HOME ALREADY!
GOT IT!

KAIDOU.
WHAT'S UP?
DON'T ADD ANY MORE. IT'S DISGUSTING.
YES, SIIIIR.
(Empty words.)
CHAK
THOSE EARS! IT'S TOO MUCH!
Huh?
BUT THEY'RE COOL, RIGHT?
IT'S NONE OF YOUR DAMN BUSINESS.
...
YOU'VE ADDED MORE EARRINGS.
FEH!
YUP, TWO MORE IN THE CARTILAGE.
YAY YAY
EARRINGS, HUH?
Each ear has...
...seven!
Four-teen total!!
OOH! YOU INTERESTED? I'LL PIERCE YOURS.
THOSE LOVELY VIRGIN EARS OF YOURS, SOU.
YAY
LOOK AT THOSE PRETTY EARS.
YOU'VE NEVER PUT HOLES IN THEM, HAVE YOU?
NOT IN MY EARS.
WHAAAT? WHAT'S THAT?! SOUNDS LIKE A DEEP, DARK SECRET!
THEN WHERE DO YOU HAVE HOLES, YOU KINKY BOY?
DON'T GET ALL EXCITED.
SO FOR EARRINGS, DO YOU USE A NEEDLE OR SOME-THING?

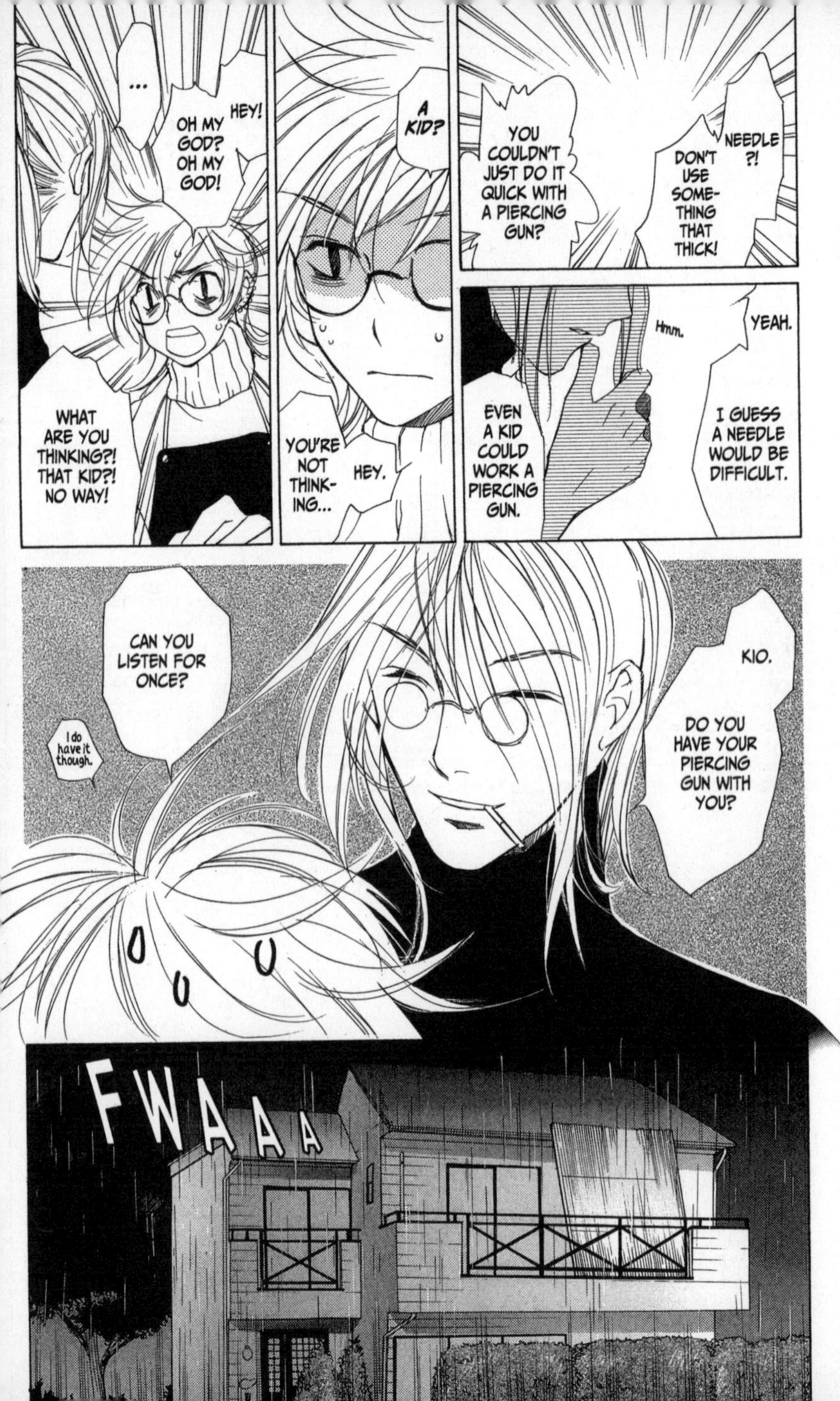
NEEDLE?!
DON'T USE SOMETHING THAT THICK!
YOU COULDN'T JUST DO IT QUICK WITH A PIERCING GUN?
YEAH.
Hmm.
I GUESS A NEEDLE WOULD BE DIFFICULT.
EVEN A KID COULD WORK A PIERCING GUN.
A KID?
HEY.
YOU'RE NOT THINKING...
HEY!
...
OH MY GOD? OH MY GOD!
WHAT ARE YOU THINKING?! THAT KID?! NO WAY!
KIO.
DO YOU HAVE YOUR PIERCING GUN WITH YOU?
CAN YOU LISTEN FOR ONCE?
I do have it though.
FWAAA

CHING

I USED TO THINK...

...BUDDHIST ALTARS...

...WERE SCARY, BUT NOW I THINK THEY'RE BEAUTIFUL.

THE PURE WHITE CHRYSANTHEMUMS...

THE LIGHT OF THE CANDLE...

IT'S ALL SO BEAUTIFUL.

RIT-SUKA.

DINNER TIME.

COMING!

CLINK
CLINK
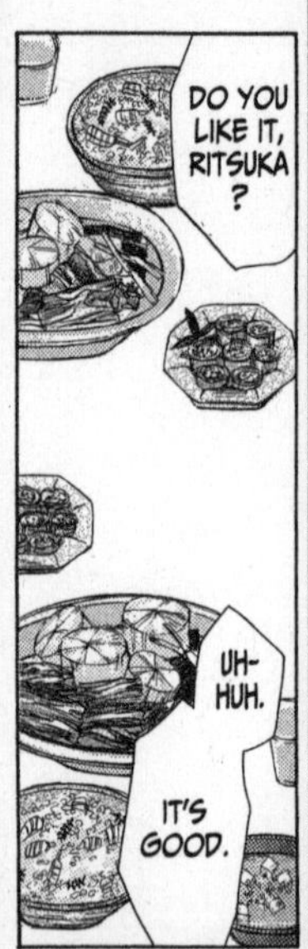
DO YOU LIKE IT, RITSUKA?
UH-HUH.
IT'S GOOD.

TWITCH
OH...

...
OOPS, DID I JUST STEP ON A LANDMINE?
I...
...don't know.
MNCH
MNCH

WHAT'S THE RIGHT ANSWER?

WHAT DOES MOM WANT ME TO SAY?

HOW WOULD "RITSUKA"...

...HAVE EATEN THIS...?
I just...
...don't know.

DON'T TRY TO FIND THE RIGHT ANSWER.
THERE'S NO SUCH THING.
YOU'RE FINE JUST THE WAY YOU ARE, RITSUKA.
BUT SEIMEI, YOU'RE WRONG!!
THIS ISN'T RITSUKA...
STOP IT, MOTHER.
THAT ATTITUDE OF YOURS ONLY PUTS MORE PRESSURE ON RITSUKA.
BUT...
SEIMEI... I...
STOP IT! STOP IT!
DON'T CALL HIM RITSUKA!
HE'S NOT RITSUKA.
MOTHER!!
CALM DOWN...
AND YOU, SEIMEI! WHEN DID YOU BECOME LIKE THIS?!
WHY WON'T YOU LISTEN TO ME?!
MISAKI...
SEIMEI, YOU TOO.
KNOCK IT OFF.
DAD!!
DON'T YOU FEEL BAD FOR YOUR MOTHER?
IT'S ALL RIGHT, MISAKI.

IT'S ALL RIGHT.
YOU! YOU COULD NEVER UNDER-STAND...

DON'T LET IT GET TO YOU.

YOU HAVEN'T DONE ANYTHING WRONG, RITSUKA.

I DO EVERYTHING I CAN.
BUT WHY IS THERE SUCH A BIG DIFFERENCE...

...BETWEEN THE "RITSUKA" OF TWO YEARS AGO...
...AND ME, RIGHT NOW?
UH.
!!
FLINCH
W-WHAT?
UH, WELL...
I MEANT TO TELL YOU TOMORROW IS PARENTS' DAY AT SCHOOL.
WE'RE SO DIFFERENT ON THE INSIDE.

WE LOOK THE SAME ON THE OUTSIDE...
...BUT FROM MOTHER'S POINT OF VIEW...
WHO... WHAT?
WHO'S SUPPOSED TO GO?
TWITCH
TWITCH
DAD, I THINK.
THAT'S IMPOSSIBLE. HE HAS WORK.
NO WAY!
I GUESS IT MAKES IT EVEN WORSE FOR HER.

I'M SORRY.
YEAH, I FIGURED.
YOU DON'T HAVE TO COME.
I have good grades anyway.

I'M SORRY.

ZWEEE

TAK

HERE'S SEIMEI'S COMPUTER.

OKAY.

INFORMATION ABOUT SEPTIMAL MOON...

....SHOULD BE INSIDE.

THIS IS THE PROBLEM.

AT LEAST...
...I THOUGHT IT WOULD BE.
Not here.
Not here.
I'VE BEEN CHECKING FOR BACKUP DISKS TOO.
SIGH...

KREE

"CALL ME ANY TIME."
...
"A PERFECTLY GOOD REASON."
"SO THAT YOU'RE NEVER LONELY, RITSUKA."

FWAAAA
STARE
A WATCHED PHONE NEVER RINGS.

BDMP
DRIP
IF YOU WANT TO HEAR MY VOICE...
...YOU SHOULD JUST CALL ME.
I DON'T.
FWAP
WHY DO YOU ALWAYS COME IN THROUGH THE WINDOW?!
THAT'S NOT AN ENTRANCE!
THEN WHY LEAVE IT UNLOCKED?
YOU HOPE THAT I'M COMING, DON'T YOU?
CHAK
WELL, TODAY...

I HAVE A FAVOR TO ASK YOU, RITSUKA.
WHAT ...?
BUT FIRST...
...DRY YOURSELF OFF.
YOU'LL CATCH A COLD!
I don't believe it.
No umbrella?
Use an umbrella!
LOOK.
IT'S A BEAUTIFUL EAR, ISN'T IT?
AND NOW...

I WANT YOU TO PUNCH A HOLE IN IT.
...
What?
ERK
WHAT?!
Punch a hole?
THAT'S RIGHT.
PIERCE IT.
MAKE ME YOURS, RITSUKA.
HERE.
WUP
I FIGURE THAT USING A NEEDLE WOULD BE TOO MUCH, SO I BROUGHT THIS.
WOOO
Titanium Long Type
Hypo-allergenic
Sterilized Piercing Device
Stainless steel piercing
WHAT?!
YOU WANT ME TO PIERCE YOU?! PUNCH A HOLE?! ME?!
NO WAY!
I CAN'T DO THAT!!
YOU CAN.
JUST HOLD IT HERE.
NO!
I MEAN... YOUR EARS...
IT'S YOUR BODY! YOUR BODY!

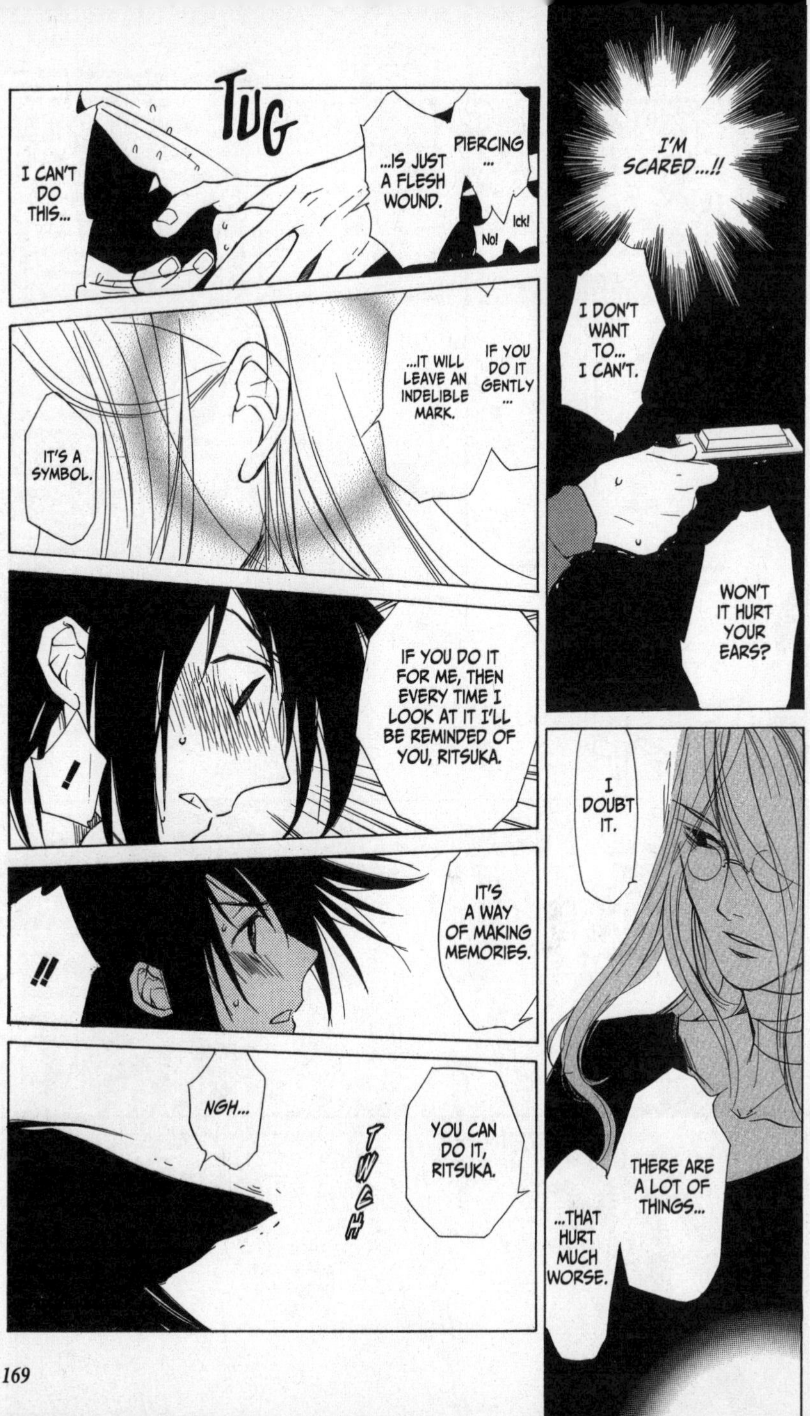

I'M SCARED...!!
I DON'T WANT TO... I CAN'T.
WON'T IT HURT YOUR EARS?

I DOUBT IT.
THERE ARE A LOT OF THINGS...
...THAT HURT MUCH WORSE.

PIERCING ...
...IS JUST A FLESH WOUND.
Ick!
No!
TUG
I CAN'T DO THIS...

IF YOU DO IT GENTLY ...
...IT WILL LEAVE AN INDELIBLE MARK.
IT'S A SYMBOL.

IF YOU DO IT FOR ME, THEN EVERY TIME I LOOK AT IT I'LL BE REMINDED OF YOU, RITSUKA.
!

IT'S A WAY OF MAKING MEMORIES.
!!

YOU CAN DO IT, RITSUKA.
TWICH
NGH...

THAT'S IT. RIGHT THERE.
CHRK
Ngh!
No!
Ears are so soft ...
SWF
BE FIRM.
HEH
IF YOU DON'T PUNCH THE HOLE QUICK AND CLEAN...
...IT'LL HURT A LOT MORE.
Hm?
OH.
GOT IT.
THEN GO AHEAD AND ENJOY THE PAIN!
!
HCHOK

NGH...
STING
NEXT!
WHIP
THE LEFT EAR!
NGH!
CHOK
DOES IT HURT?
SHAKE
SHAKE
NO.
HUFF
SOUBI... DO YOU LIKE PAIN?
PEOPLE LIKE THAT ARE CALLED "MASOCHISTS."
SHAKE
SHAKE

NO.
I HATE PAIN.
HE LOOKS SO CALM...
YOU'RE ALWAYS LYING.
THANK YOU, RITSUKA.
THIS MAKES ME HAPPY.

SLUMP
THEN...
OBEY ME.
I WILL.
ASK ANY-THING.

THERE'S ONLY ONE THING I WANT.
FIND THE PEOPLE WHO KILLED SEIMEI...!

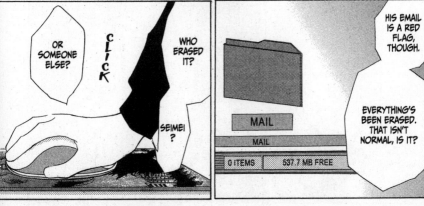

FZZZT
TAK TAK
ZZT ZZT
THERE'S ONLY THIS ONE MESSAGE ABOUT SEPTIMAL MOON.
"I WILL BE KILLED BY SEPTIMAL MOON."
I CHECKED EVERY-WHERE IN THE COMPUTER AND THROUGH HIS OLD DISKS...
...BUT THERE'S NOTHING ELSE.
HIS EMAIL IS A RED FLAG, THOUGH.
EVERYTHING'S BEEN ERASED. THAT ISN'T NORMAL, IS IT?
MAIL
MAIL
0 ITEMS
537.7 MB FREE
WHO ERASED IT?
SEIMEI?
CLICK
OR SOMEONE ELSE?

SOUBI.

YOU...

YOU KNOW SOMETHING ABOUT SEPTIMAL MOON, DON'T YOU?

TELL ME!

SHAKE

I CAN'T.

SNAP

What?!

WHY YOU...!!

DAMMIT!

YOU SAID TO ASK ANYTHING!

ON THAT PARTICULAR SUBJECT, I HAVE ORDERS FROM HIGHER UP.

I AM NOT ALLOWED TO ANSWER QUESTIONS PERTAINING TO SEPTIMAL MOON.

WHY NOT?

I JUST CAN'T.

IF YOU ARE NOT PLEASED, RITSUKA...

MRGH

...FEEL FREE...

...TO PUNISH ME.

GET OUT OF HERE!
SKRUT
I DON'T WANT TO SEE YOUR FACE!

SHFF

PLOK
IT'S RAINING...
...OUT THERE.
FWAAAA
YOU'LL GET WET.
RITSUKA...
DON'T CALL ME.
I DON'T WANT TO SEE YOU.
I... I'M SICK OF THINKING ABOUT YOU ALL THE TIME, SOUBI.

RITSUKA...
YOU THINK ABOUT ME ALL THE TIME?
HE'S DOING IT AGAIN, KILLING ME WITH SWEET WORDS.

OF COURSE I DO.
IT...
IT'S EXHAUSTING!

I WANT TO SEE YOU.

I DON'T WANT TO SEE YOU.

I LOVE YOU, RITSUKA.

TOMORROW'S PARENTS' DAY, RIGHT?
SHALL I GO FOR YOU?
FLICK
!!
HOW DID YOU KNOW...?
I TALKED TO YUIKO ON THE PHONE.
IF YOU WANT ME TO LISTEN TO YOU...
NO WAY, SOUBI...
I DON'T WANT YOU TO COME!
REALLY?
OF COURSE NOT!!
COM-MAND ME.
PLEASE ...
RITSUKA.
MAKE IT AN ORDER.

GO...
GO HOME ALREADY!
DON'T COME TO PARENTS' DAY!!!
IF YOU UNDERSTAND, THEN GO HOME!
... I UNDERSTAND.
FWAAA
I'LL GO HOME.
CHAK
THANK YOU.
FOR THE UM-BRELLA.
GOOD NIGHT.
FWAP
SOUBI ...

DON'T GET WET.
DON'T CATCH A COLD.
THAT'S ...
...AN ORDER!
YES, SIR.
FWAAAA

PWEEP PWEEP PWEEP PWEEP

BIP

HELLO?

HI, YUIKO.

GOOD EVENING.

HEH HEH HEH. GOOD EVENING.

I CALLED YA!

OH, IS THIS SOUBI?

IT'S YUIKO. ♡

IT'S RAINING, ISN'T IT?

YES.

DID YOU ALREADY TAKE A BATH?

NOT YET. WHAT ABOUT YOU, YUIKO?

I DID. FOR TWO HOURS!

THAT'S A LONG TIME.

BUT...!

I ADMIRE YOU, RITSUKA.

FOR YOUR STRENGTH.

Y'KNOW, TOMORROW'S PARENTS' DAY!!

REALLY.

MY DADDY CAN'T COME.

BUT RITSUKA SAID HIS PARENTS COULDN'T COME EITHER.

...

...

WHAT'S THE MATTER?

IS THERE SOMETHING YOU WANT TO SAY?

...

...

IT...

IT DOESN'T MATTER...

...IF YOU'RE TALL OR SHORT...

DOES IT...?

I LOVE YOU.

IT'S SILLY TO WORRY ABOUT HOW TALL...

...OR SHORT YOU ARE, RIGHT?

IT'S NOT SILLY AT ALL.

DOES IT BOTHER YOU, YUIKO?

SOB

SNIFF...

SOB...

SNIFF...

WAAAHH!!

SOB

DON'T CRY.

FROM MY PERSPECTIVE...

...YOU'RE VERY PETITE, YUIKO. YOU'RE SO CUTE.

SOB

HUH...

REALLY?

SOB

I SWEAR.

AND BESIDES, I THINK RITSUKA WILL GROW UP AND BE TALLER THAN YOU IN NO TIME, YUIKO.

REALLY?

I SWEAR.

RITSUKA'S OLDER BROTHER WAS TALL, AFTER ALL.

SOUBI.
IF I WERE EVER TO DIE, YOU WOULD THEN BELONG TO RITSUKA.
AFFIRMATIVE.

SEIMEI TOLD ME TO...
SO I WENT TO RITSUKA.

BUT I HAD NO IDEA...
...THAT HE WOULD BE LIKE THIS.

I HAD NO IDEA...
...THAT I WOULD GROW TO LOVE HIM SO MUCH.
CHIRP
CHIRP

Papers: Big Sky, Starry Sky; Shooting Star

BONG
THANK YOU TO ALL THE PARENTS...
...WHO MADE TIME IN THEIR BUSY SCHEDULES TO JOIN US TODAY.

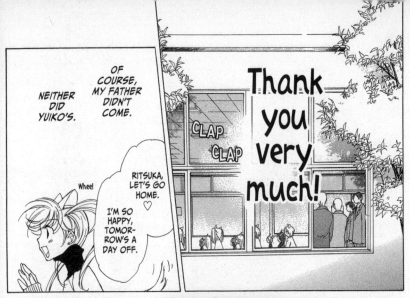

Thank you very much!
CLAP
CLAP
OF COURSE, MY FATHER DIDN'T COME.
NEITHER DID YUIKO'S.
RITSUKA, LET'S GO HOME. ♡
I'M SO HAPPY, TOMORROW'S A DAY OFF.
Whee!

YOU TWO AREN'T DATING, RIGHT?
RIGHT.
Uh... uh-huh.
THEN I CAN'T GIVE UP ON YUIKO.
I DON'T MIND STARTING OUT AS FRIENDS.
AND I WANT TO GET TO KNOW YOU BETTER, AOYAGI.
HMPH
ME?
What a weirdo.
YOU WANT TO MAKE MEMORIES WITH ME?
Weird!
?
?
MEMO-RIES?
SOME-THING LIKE THAT...I GUESS.
What?
PERK
I SEE.
I SEE!
Okay!
SO YOU WANT TO MAKE MEMORIES.
LET'S DO IT!
OKAY. THEN...
YUIKO WANTS TO GO TO KINUTA PARK.
WHAT'S HIS DEAL?
VRRRT

BDMP...

AOYAGI, YOUR PHONE'S RINGING.
VRRRRT
UH...
YEAH.

I'LL BET IT'S SOUBI.
VRR...
WHO?
UH...

HE'S RITSUKA'S... UH... SERVANT?
I THINK?
Servant...?

SORRY!
DASH
I'LL CALL YOU ABOUT TOMORROW LATER!
HUH? HUH?
OKAAAY!

HUFF
SOUBI!
YES?
WHA...
WHAT ARE YOU DOING HERE?!
YOU DIDN'T TELL ME NOT TO COME PICK YOU UP.
CHK
AND YOU DIDN'T TELL ME TO NEVER COME SEE YOU AGAIN EITHER.
BY THE WAY...
...YOU ALSO NEVER TOLD ME NOT TO LOVE YOU, RITSUKA.
OR ARE YOU GOING TO FORBID THAT FROM NOW ON TOO?

...
WHAT-EVER.
FEH!
THEN...
SHALL WE GO?
OKAY...
BLUSH
I WAS THINKING WE COULD TAKE MORE PICTURES TODAY.
SOUNDS GOOD!
MY FRIEND SWIPED ALL THE PICTURES FROM BEFORE.
?
I'LL PRINT OUT ANOTHER SET.
THANK YOU, RITSUKA! I LOVE YOU.
LOVELESS 1 / END

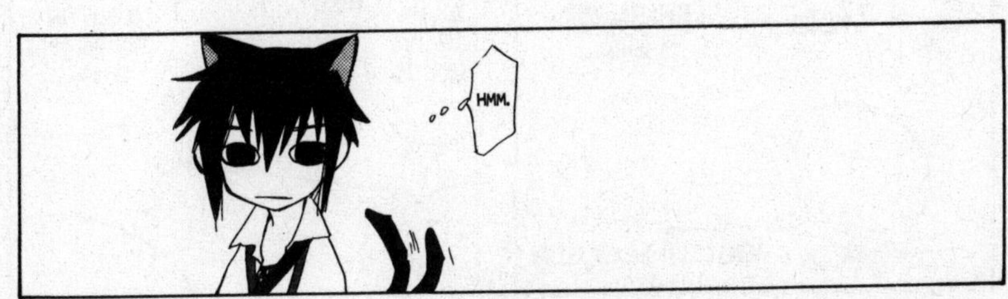
HMM.

PANEL BORDER
INSERT PAGE NUMBERS HERE
THIS IS MY SPECIALIZED THUMBNAIL PAPER. IT'S REALLY CONVENIENT TO USE. B5 SIZE.
Backstage epilogue, starring the manga artist and editor
Yun Kouga
Loveless begins!
CLAP
CLAP
CLAP
CLAP
So.
About the blurb for *Loveless.*
Yes.
Like a sheep
MANGA ARTIST
In Profile
EDITOR S
SCRIPT
How about "This time Yun Kouga gets serious!"
You like it?
Hey, now!
First of all, I'm always serious.
I am!
You mean you're serious about goofing off, or being a serious pain in the butt?
WHAAAT?
Do you want to die?
Oh no!
It's start-ing!
!!
ULP!
THUMB-NAILS
Thank you for buying *Loveless* volume 1.
I'll work hard, so please give us your support!!
Layout
KANJI CHARACTER QUIZ
ZZZZZ...
I love you, sleep.
USING CELL PHONE AS A PILLOW

!!
PWEEP
PWEEP
PWEEP
PWEEP
Hello, this is Kouga.
You were sleeping, weren't you?
Of course not.
Why do you lie?
BDMP
BDMP
BDMP
After lunch you said you needed to take a walk for a change of pace, and went to buy some books and drink tea and then after getting back you slept for two hours and after taking a shower and eating a snack you went to sleep again, didn't you?
...
SHUFF
SHUFF
RSTL
It's no use. I've hidden the camera in a place where you'll never find it.
You stalker!!
Pervert!!
You slow-poke!! Slacker!!
You always miss deadlines!! Liar!! You have no marketable skills other than drawing manga, so get cracking!!
GRR
GRR
GRR
GRR
Please, I'm asking nicely.
I'm really looking forward to your pages.
SEA OF BLOOD
Now you know the wonderful, collaborative atmosphere in which *Loveless* is created.
We hope you support us for a long time.
• www.ichijinsha.co.jp ← Home Page
• www.kokonoe.com ← my website
I hope you read volume 2 as well!
NOT THE WINGS OF AN ANGEL, BUT OF A FLY!!

I feel like I've changed a bit since starting work on *Loveless*. How so? You'll have to read on and see for yourself!

—Yun Kouga, 2002

loveless_yunkouga_2002_comic:zerosum_ichijinsha

The following content ran as a SPECIAL LIMITED EDITION BOOKLET sold with Loveless volume 1.

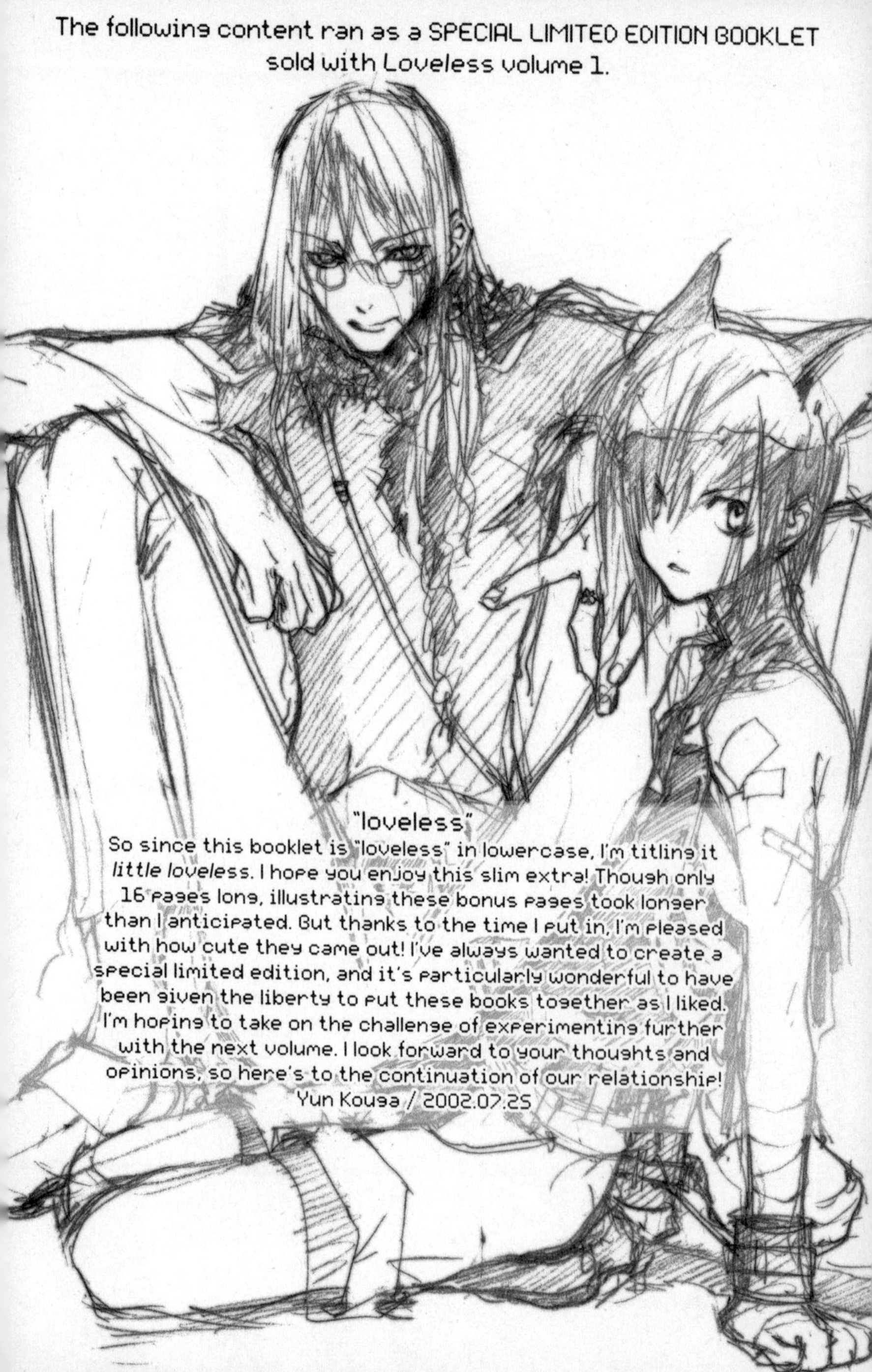

"loveless"

So since this booklet is "loveless" in lowercase, I'm titling it *little loveless*. I hope you enjoy this slim extra! Though only 16 pages long, illustrating these bonus pages took longer than I anticipated. But thanks to the time I put in, I'm pleased with how cute they came out! I've always wanted to create a special limited edition, and it's particularly wonderful to have been given the liberty to put these books together as I liked. I'm hoping to take on the challenge of experimenting further with the next volume. I look forward to your thoughts and opinions, so here's to the continuation of our relationship!

Yun Kouga / 2002.07.25

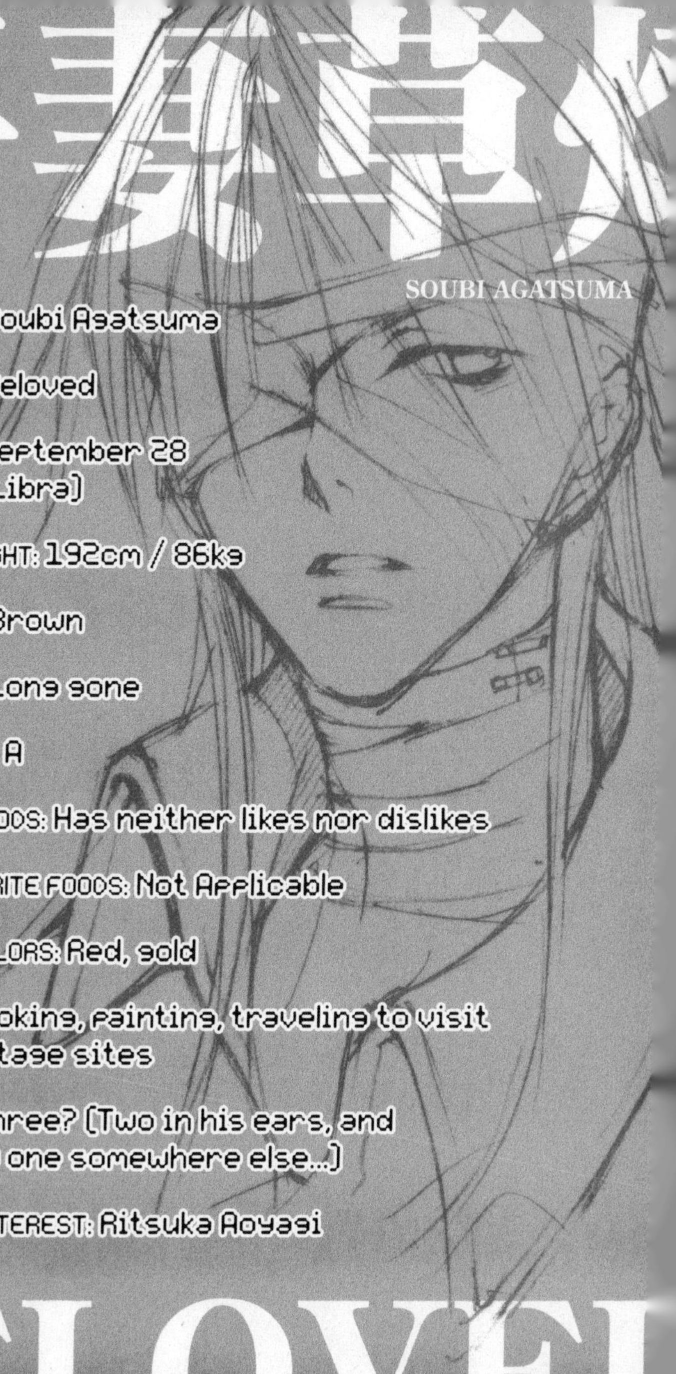

吾妻

SOUBI AGATSUMA

- NAME_01: Soubi Agatsuma
- NAME_02: Beloved
- BIRTHDAY: September 28 (Libra)
- HEIGHT/WEIGHT: 192cm / 86kg
- EYES/HAIR: Brown
- EARS/TAIL: Long gone
- BLOOD TYPE: A
- FAVORITE FOODS: Has neither likes nor dislikes
- LEAST FAVORITE FOODS: Not Applicable
- FAVORITE COLORS: Red, gold
- HOBBIES: Cooking, painting, traveling to visit world heritage sites
- PIERCINGS: Three? (Two in his ears, and apparently one somewhere else...)
- PERSON OF INTEREST: Ritsuka Aoyagi

BELOVE

青柳立夏
RITSUKA AOYAGI
● NAME_01: Ritsuka Aoyagi
● NAME_02: Loveless
● BIRTHDAY: December 12 (Sagittarius)
● HEIGHT/WEIGHT: 147cm / 31kg
● EYES/HAIR: Black
● EARS/TAIL: Present
● BLOOD TYPE: B
● FAVORITE FOODS: Soft foods, anything from McDonald's, convenience store rice ball bentos
● LEAST FAVORITE FOODS: Too many to name, very picky eater
● FAVORITE COLORS: Shades of blue, white
● HOBBIES: Making memories
● PIERCINGS: None
● PERSON OF INTEREST: Soubi Agatsuma
LOVELESS

SUGINO vs. KOUGA

Wa ha ha! Master Sugi mentioned that he dislikes writing by hand, so I blackmailed him into doing it.♡

Kouga: Hello!! Kouga here!! (I'm the manga artist!!) Today I'll be chatting with my editor.

⪢Applause!⪡

Sugino: Hhhhello! I'm Editor Sugino... I've never done something like this before, so I'm really nervous... Pleased to be here.

Ⓚ: Editing is a really tough job, isn't it? Especially when you get coerced into stuff like this. By the way, no corrections allowed.

Ⓢ: I mean, I'm still new to this sort of work. So, uh, how's it going? Volume 1 is on sale!

Ⓚ: (Why is your handwriting getting smaller?!) So you HATE Soubi, right, Master Sugi?

Ⓢ: That's not true. Even you were saying, "He's creepy..." ...So about the graphic novels...

Ⓚ: I gave the special limited edition books my best effort. There are things I wish I could have done, bat I'll leave those for the next time!! (Don't give me a hard time!)

Ⓢ: You really did put a lot of work into them! What shall we do for the next one? ...This is a misspelling, right?

Ⓚ: We'll do another one of these conversations.

Ⓢ: ARE YOU KIDDING ME?! Writing is hard :(

Ⓚ: Says the person who remembers to bring Hanazono dumplings every day but forgot a pen for this conversation...

Ⓢ: I didn't think we were going to go through with it...Was the monaka tasty?

Ⓚ: Weak! (I'm not talking about the monaka... That was delicious.) When I say I'm going to do something, I do it. Hey, what did you think the first time you saw the storyboards for this manga?

Ⓢ: They were interesting. I thought, "Wow! This is Yun Kouga!" Although during our first meeting I did feel like I was being sexually harassed. lol

Ⓚ: (...? What about the storyboards...?) That's what you think of me?

Ⓢ: (Storyboards first, huh?) I think that you are, forgetting logic for the moment, all about coolness & cuteness & eroticism.

Ⓚ: What's with you, Master Sugi?! You're not going to tell me to die or yell that you're going to kill me today??

Ⓢ: That's all I've been saying... I wonder if you're going to stay true to form for the rest of your life in that you "can't hit deadlines"!

Ⓚ: What? But I always hit my deadlines. (There, I said it! Now, how many people will actually believe it? *FIDGET FIDGET*)

Ⓢ: Uh, sure...(deadpan) Well, you do try your best each month. (← Does she have something on me?)

Ⓚ: In any case, I'm glad that you like Loveless, Master Sugi. You do, right?

Ⓢ: I'm a big fan! Please stay interested in it. (← **his true feelings?**)

Ⓚ: Is it okay to ramp up the eroticism? (trying to secure a promise)

Ⓢ: As long as it's fun! Of course anything goes... But there are limits. Anything we have to put a censor mosaic over would be too much. (← **Oh, c'mon.**)

Ⓚ: There's nothing erotic about a mosaic. (Whuh?!) I want to get the second volume out within the year.

Ⓢ: I see, I see! Let's do our best! For as long as we live!! ...Which would be now...

Ⓚ: Master Sugi has a blog online at Zero-Sum's website, so everyone please check it out! See ya!!

Ⓢ: What the hell?! :D Well, like it or not, this is the artist of Loveless, so please favor us with your ongoing support. (← **Say what?!**)

If I die, let it be by your words.
LOVELESS
Congratulations on the release of volume 1!
The combination of "loser adult and levelheaded child" is a big-time hook for me. I totally look forward to it every month. I'm so glad to be working for *Zero-Sum*. :D
Ms. Kouga, please allow me to join you for drinks again. I'd love to talk about work with you! Thank you for asking me to contribute this guest art. It really feels like a milestone for me. But I'm sorry I couldn't make Ritsuka sufficiently cute... (sweating) Next time I hope you can draw lovely portraits of my children...!! :D
KAZUYA MINEKURA 2002

YURI NARUSHIMA
CONGRATS ON VOLUME 1!!
CLAP
CLAP
A tidbit...
Yun Kouga, embarrassed as never before, and my rude self.
One day, in Yokohama
Um, so ears... y'know, ears ...?
I was thinking about the lead in this next manga, and I thought I'd try out some ears...
After I drew some c-cat ears I couldn't stop going down that path, and it was like, what the hell, but...
Wait, but why cat ears?
Are they going to let me draw a peculiar manga like that...?
Huh?
Ms. Kouga, when have you ever drawn a manga that **wasn't** peculiar?
100% True Story

Yayyyy!!! D-did you see that?! Did you see it?!
Our guests for the commemorative first volume were Yuri Narushima and Kazuya Minekura. I'm so happy! Please continue to bless us with your kindness!
Ms. Minekura! Your portrayal of a tough, scrappy Ritsuka and the lovably pathetic loser-adult Soubi (hee hee) is just what I'd expect from you!! I promise to repay this kindness! I'm certain that it will go over big with the readers too.
I hope to see you again in volume 2.
We are published monthly in Zero-Sum, so please support the magazine as well. You must be thinking I don't have anything else to say. But hmm, I don't. A big thank-you to all you readers and to the people who helped make this!

YURI NARUSHIMA http://www.naruri.com/top.html
KAZUYA MINEKURA nitroblog.exblog.jp
YUN KOUGA http://www.kokonoe.com
ZERO-SUM / ICHIJINSHA http://www.ichijinsha.co.jp/

loveless
BLEH! NO WAY, NO WAY!!
I'M NEVER EATING FERMENTED SOY-BEANS!
HISS
HISS
ME NEITHER! NUH-UH! NOT GONNA EAT 'EM!!

I'M DUMBFOUNDED.
DUMBFOUNDED
LISTEN TO YOU TWO.
IT'S ALWAYS "CAN'T EAT THIS, CAN'T EAT THAT."
SO WHAT DO YOU DO ABOUT SCHOOL LUNCHES?
I NEVER EAT 'EM.
I NEVER EAT 'EM.
THEN WHAT *DO* YOU LIKE TO EAT?
SOFT STUFF.
Chewing's a pain.
PUDDING AND ICE CREAM. AND STRAWBERRIES TOO. ♡

ANYTHING FROM MCDONALD'S.
AND THE RICE BALL BENTO FROM 7-11.
ME TOO!
OKAY, STOP.
I'LL WHIP UP SOMETHING WITH WHATEVER'S AVAILABLE.

SZZZZL

AFTER SCHOOL...

...

...SOUBI OCCASIONALLY COOKS FOR US AT YUIKO'S HOUSE.

SZZZL

SINCE WE'RE REALLY PICKY EATERS, HE GETS KINDA MAD AT US.
Y'KNOW, SOUBI...

YOU ALWAYS SAY THAT YOU'LL DO WHATEVER I WANT.
SO WHY TRY TO FEED ME STUFF THAT I DON'T LIKE?

SO YOU'LL GROW UP INTO A FINE ADULT.
SZZL
STARE

WHAT'S THAT MEAN?
THAT'S GOT NOTHING TO DO WITH FOOD.
YES, IT DOES.
AT THIS RATE YOU'RE NOT GOING TO GROW ANY TALLER.
HRMPH!
LIAR!

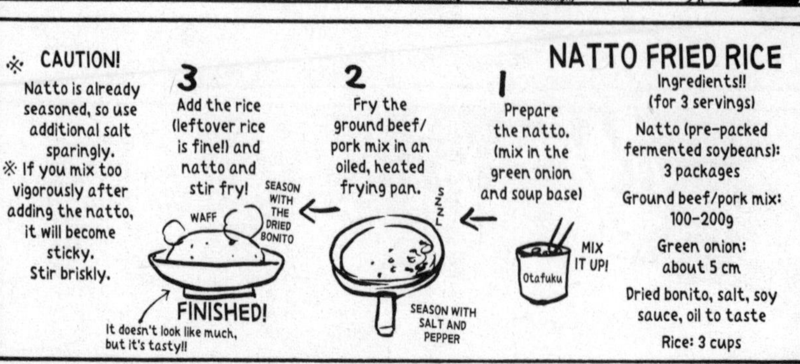
NATTO FRIED RICE
Ingredients!!
(for 3 servings)
Natto (pre-packed fermented soybeans): 3 packages
Ground beef/pork mix: 100-200g
Green onion: about 5 cm
Dried bonito, salt, soy sauce, oil to taste
Rice: 3 cups
1
Prepare the natto. (mix in the green onion and soup base)
MIX IT UP!
Otafuku
2
Fry the ground beef/pork mix in an oiled, heated frying pan.
SZZL
SEASON WITH SALT AND PEPPER
3
Add the rice (leftover rice is fine!) and natto and stir fry!
SEASON WITH THE DRIED BONITO
WAFF
FINISHED!
It doesn't look like much, but it's tasty!!
※ CAUTION!
Natto is already seasoned, so use additional salt sparingly.
※ If you mix too vigorously after adding the natto, it will become sticky. Stir briskly.

WHAT ABOUT ASPARAGUS?
I HATE IT!!
I HATE VEGETABLES.
BUT WHY?
GRRR!
IT'S JUST FATE!!
I DON'T GET IT...

BUT YOU LIKE TUNA, RIGHT?
TURN
I'LL ADD THIS, SO EAT UP.
ULP!
BARF!
DON'T MIX UP STUFF I LIKE WITH STUFF I HATE!

GREEN SALAD

Ingredients!!
Anything green is OK.

- Cucumbers
- Broad beans
- Asparagus
- Green soybeans
- Peas
- Green beans
- Can of tuna fish (spicy!)

Do Steps 1 and 2 at the same time.

1. Cut up the vegetables.
Use a slicer for the cucumbers.

2. Boil:
Asparagus: 1–2 minutes is good.

•Broad beans:
If you make an incision in the middle with a knife, they won't shrink when you boil them.

•Green soybeans:
← CUT HERE
You can cut them up using scissors, like they do in fine restaurants (ha ha).
Boil to semi-hardness.

Boil in a small amount of water for 5 to 6 minutes!! You can also add wakame seaweed and onions.

3. Dress everything with the spicy tuna.
If you like, you can squeeze in a lemon.
If you don't have the spicy kind of tuna, add a bit of soy sauce and Chinese chili oil.

DO YOU LIKE MISO SOUP?
I DO...
WHY'S THAT?
BECAUSE OF THE DRIED SARDINES IN IT...

MISO SOUP WITH BEAN SPROUTS AND DEEP-FRIED BEAN CURD

If making soup stock with dried sardines, it's fine to remove the head and stomach.

It's just a simple miso soup with bean sprouts and deep-fried bean curd.

The one point to consider:
Prepare a regular deep-fried bean curd miso soup, and top it off with bean sprouts stir-fried in sesame oil!!

Delicious!

But don't simmer the bean sprouts in the miso soup.

NO WAY!
I CAN'T EAT NATTO FRIED RICE.
YOU'LL BE FINE.

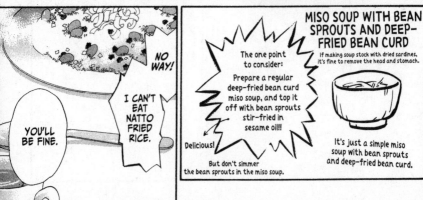

IT'S GOT DRIED BONITO IN IT!
NGH...
NO
JUST HUMOR ME, AND TRY ONE BITE.
!
CHOMP
...
...
...
MUNSCH MUNSCH
!!
IT'S GOOD!

SO HOW DID YOU KNOW...
...THAT I LIKED DRIED BONITO?

JUST A HUNCH.
BECAUSE SOME-ONE'S JUST A LITTLE KITTY AT HEART.

THERE'S DESSERT TOO. TOFU JELLY.
POK
SKRUT
THERE'S NO WAY I COULD EVER EAT THAT!
JUST HEARING ABOUT IT SOUNDS GROSS!

TOFU JELLY

Ingredients:
- gelatin
- milk
- silken tofu
- sugar

1. Blend the tofu in a blender!!
2. Melt the gelatin in warm milk.
3. Mix in the blended tofu, season with sugar, and chill!!

It's even better if you have a cute mold to put it in! A drizzle of honey goes well on top.

It works with soy milk too!

IT'S SUPER TASTY.
WHO KNEW?
NGH...
THERE'S ENOUGH FOR SECONDS.

IT'S STRANGE THAT SOUBI CAN PREPARE FOOD SO EASILY AT SOMEONE ELSE'S HOUSE.

AND HE DOESN'T HAVE EARS... SOMETIMES I REMEMBER HE'S "ONE OF THEM"...
SWIP
SWIP

WE HAVE TO RESTORE THE KITCHEN BACK TO THE WAY IT WAS.
IF HER MOM FINDS OUT, WE'LL GET IN TROUBLE.
SOME-TIMES HE FEELS LIKE "ONE OF US"...
RUSTLE
RUSTLE

I THINK SOUBI LIKES PRETTY THINGS.
THAT'S VERY PRETTY.

I'M IN THE ARTS AND CRAFTS CLUB.
WE'RE MAKING CELL PHONE CHARMS.
SO... YOUR CELL PHONE LOOKS BARE, RITSUKA.
ME ?!
Leave me...
...out of this.
FLICK FLICK
YOU'RE PRETTY GOOD!
I'M JUST PUTTING BEADS ON A STRING.
BUT THE COLORS ARE NICE.
YOU HAVE GOOD COLOR SENSE, YUIKO.
HUUUH? REALLY ?
DON'T JUST PRAISE EVERYTHING!!
That's too nice.

BLUNT
YOU DON'T NEED TO SAY EVERY-THING!
BUT THAT'S WHAT I THINK.
SHOULDN'T YOU SAY WHAT YOU FEEL?

AWW...
YOU'RE A TOUGH CUSTOMER, RITSUKA.
!!
FEH!

DRIP
DRIP
DRIP
DRIP

SMILE

RITSUKA, RITSUKA!
...SHUT UP.
FLK
FLK
FLK

C'MON, RITSUKA. RITSUKA!
WHAT DO YOU WANT?!

HERE.

RITSUKA

THE BACK OF A CALENDAR

GRRR

WHAT THE HELL IS THIS?!

I THOUGHT YOU WERE AN ARTIST!

I *AM* AN ARTIST.

LIAR!

FWAAAAA
IT'S RAINING SUPER HARD.
WANNA TAKE AN UMBRELLA?
FWAA
SORRY, THE FIRST RULE OF YUIKO'S HOUSE...
...IS TO LEAVE NO TRACE OF OUR PRES-ENCE.
WE'LL BE FINE LIKE THIS.
SPSH
SPSH
...
MAYBE *YOU'RE* FINE, BUT...

!
TRMBL
IT'S PRETTY...
...CHILLY.
ARE YOU STILL COLD?
IT'S WARM.
...
SOUBI'S BODY.
DON'T CLING TO ME.
YOU'RE ALL HOT.
I WONDER WHAT...
YOU LOOK COLD-BLOODED.
SO WHY ARE YOU SO HOT?
...YOU CALL SOMETHING LIKE THIS?

YOU SAID YOU WERE COLD, RIGHT?
SKWEEZ
Every-one always says it's nice...
...that I run so hot.
I DON'T LIKE IT.
YOU'RE HOT.
AHH, I KNOW.
LIKE A HAMSTER.
IT'S LIKE THAT TIME I HELD A HAMSTER IN THE PALM OF MY HAND.
SO WARM AND SOFT.

FWAAA
IT'S KIND OF A NICE FEELING...
SO NICE THAT I COULD CRY.

little loveless 1 / END

LOVELESS

YUN:KOUGA_LOVELESS_2003

PUNISHMENT DOMINATION CRUELTY

HEY!

SOU, YOU'VE GOT PIERCINGS!

YOU WENT AND DID IT! WHEN'D THAT HAPPEN?

YOU LOOK GOOD.

THEY'RE KINDA GAY. ♥

WHY ARE YOU PERKY SO EARLY IN THE MORNING, KIO?

'CAUSE I'M A MORNING PERSON. ♥

YOU REALLY LIKE BUTTERFLIES DON'T YOU, SOU? YOU ALWAYS HAVE THEM AROUND.

BUTTER-FLIES?

TOY'S MASTER / THE ABSOLUTE TOY MASTER CHAPTERS

CHAPTER 1

TOY

"Toy"
—*noun.* An instrument of play; an object of amusement; a plaything; a person or thing to be played with for the purpose of enjoyment.

COERCE

"Coerce"
—*verb.* To compel obedience through the threat of force; to dominate or control.

ABSOLUTE

"Absolute" (definition • uses)
—*noun.* Having no equal; having no comparison; a state of perfection; a state of supremacy; to rely on nothing; to face no limitation; unconditional. *Philosophical:* An absolute being
—*adverb:* Absolutely; unconditionally; certainly; by any means.

I HATE THEM.

...
UH.
I SEE.
BUT...
...YOU'RE PAINTING BUTTERFLIES RIGHT NOW, AREN'T YOU?
WHAT'S THERE TO HATE? THEY'RE BEAUTIFUL.
I HATE THAT THEY'RE BEAUTIFUL.

NO ONE CARES ABOUT CATCHING HAIRY CATERPILLARS.
AND I HATE THE FACT THAT THEY'RE SO EASILY TRAPPED.
IS IT SO EASY?
IT'S AWFUL HOW THEY WIND UP AS SPECIMENS WITH PINS STUCK THROUGH THEIR ABDOMENS.
Whoa, touchy subject.
BUT THAT'S NOT THE BUTTERFLY'S FAULT...
I DON'T GET YOU, SOU. YOU'RE NOT MAKING SENSE.
DID SOMETHING HAPPEN?
SHUP
AH!
SOME-THING DID HAPPEN!
BDMP
TELL ME!
BDMP

WHOA, HOLD ON A SEC.

HEY.

JUST WHO EXACTLY PIERCED YOUR EARS FOR YOU?

RITSUKA.

SNAP! JUST LIKE THAT.

BARF!

WHUH ?!

GYAAAH!

YOU MADE A LITTLE VIRGIN KID DO IT!

YOU MONSTER !

I FEEL BAD FOR THE KID.

PLICH

MAN, OH MAN...
NO MORE PERVERTS FOR ME TODAY.
I'M GOING TO MY PART-TIME JOB.
SHUF...
HAVE FUN.
OHH HOO! ♥
DID I TELL YOU ABOUT MY NEW GIG?
I HAVE TO DO CRAZY THINGS IN THE NUDE IN FRONT OF A WHOLE CROWD OF PEOPLE.
RUB RUB
I'M SURE YOU'RE SPECTACULAR AT IT.

HANG ON... WHAT'S THAT SUPPOSED TO MEAN?
WHUMP

SOU, YOU REALLY DON'T GIVE A DAMN ABOUT ME, DO YOU?!
GRR
GRR
YOU SURE ACT LIKE YOU COULDN'T CARE LESS!
I WOULDN'T MIND SEEING YOU NAKED, KIO.
GRR

YOU'RE AN ART MODEL, RIGHT?

I'D LOVE TO DRAW YOU.

DAR-LING!

I'D TAKE OFF MY CLOTHES FOR YOU ANYTIME!

WHEE WHEE

WHEE

I'M GOOD.

GET TO YOUR JOB.

BIP BIP BIP

BIP BIP

BIP

BIP BIP

MMRGH
BIP BIP
BIP
BIP BIP

SHUF

TOK.
MORNING, SEIMEI.
YOU'RE RELIEVED THAT SEIMEI'S DEAD, AREN'T YOU?

MISAKI ... WHY WOULD YOU SAY THAT?
I'M NOT DUMB!

YOU'RE PATHETIC.
WHAT A MISERABLE MAN.
SEIMEI WAS STRONGER THAN YOU'LL EVER BE.

MOM CALLED SEIMEI STRONG.

SEIMEI WAS SO MUCH MORE OF A MAN THAN YOU ARE.

STOP TRYING TO STIR THINGS UP.

SEIMEI WAS SUPPOSED TO PROTECT ME.

BUT THE SEIMEI I KNEW WAS KIND.

JUST LIKE MOM.

SEIMEI WAS GOING TO...
...TAKE ME AWAY FROM THIS PLACE!!
BAM
BAM
ME AND... RITSUKA ...
BUT NOW HE'S DEAD. IT'S ALL OVER!!
BAM

...IT'S OVER?
BUT...
AT THE FUNERAL, THE PRIEST SAID DEATH WASN'T THE END.

SEIMEI IS STILL "HERE."
IF I LIGHT INCENSE EVERY DAY...
...AND PRAY...
MY MEMORY OF HIM IS SO VIVID.
... HE'LL HEAR ME.

...
ARE YOU STUPID?
IT'S OVER!!
OVER!!
CRASH
WHEN YOU DIE, THAT'S THE END!!

WHAP
!
NOTHING STAYS BEHIND!
HE CAN'T DO ANYTHING ANYMORE!
VSH
MOTHER!
GLUNK
LOOK!

YANK
LOOK!
WHAT CAN SEIMEI DO FOR YOU NOW?!
M...!
HE WON'T SAVE YOU!
NOBODY IS COMING TO SAVE YOU!

WHAT'S YOUR PROBLEM?
YOU'RE RUNNING AWAY?!
YOU'RE NOT GOING TO STOP ME?
YOU HAVE TO STOP ME!!
KLAT
I WON'T MOVE.
I CAN'T PROVOKE HER...SHE'LL ONLY HIT ME AGAIN...
SEIMEI'S DEAD!
HE'S GONE!
!!
HE CAN'T DO ANYTHING!
THAT'S WHY...
THERE'S NOBODY...
SWSH
...TO STOP ME!!

B-ING
B-ONG
THANKS, EVERYONE! THAT'S ALL FOR NOW.
ATTENTION!
BOW!
NOW MOVE ALONG TO THE MUSIC ROOM DURING THE TEN-MINUTE BREAK.
SKRUT
SKRUT
MURMUR
MURMUR
MS. SHINONOME! RITSUKA DIDN'T COME!
I WONDER WHY? IS HE JUST TARDY...?

SOME-THING MUST HAVE HAPPENED.
RITSUKA'S NEVER TARDY.

BUT...
HE'LL COME TODAY...
I KNOW HE WILL.
HE PROMISED.
FIRST DISTRICT PA
HEY, HEY! ♡
RITSUKA, GET THIS!

I'M LISTENING.
SO WE WENT TO PICK STRAW-BERRIES THIS WEEKEND.
ME, MY MOM AND DAD—THE THREE OF US!!
ALL THREE OF US, AS A FAMILY.
KREE
KREE

HUH.
MY PARENTS FINALLY GOT THE SAME DAY OFF!
KREE
KREE
KREE
THE LAST TIME I WAS IN FOURTH GRADE.
BUT STRAWBERRY SEASON WAS OVER, SO EVEN THOUGH WE WENT, THERE WERE HARDLY ANY LEFT!

WE JUST LAUGHED.
DADDY HAD BEEN SO PUMPED UP, HE WAS SO DISAPPOINTED.
THAT'S TOO BAD.
KREE
IT'S ALL GOOD!
WE COULDN'T EAT THAT MANY STRAWBERRIES, ANYWAY.
I WANTED TO EAT A HUNDRED, BUT THERE WAS NO WAY.

Yikes.
You'd get a stomachache!
THAT'S KIND OF SCARY, ACTUALLY.
YOU THINK? I GOT NICE AND FULL!
I LOVE STRAWBERRIES.
SIGH
BUT EVEN I COULDN'T EAT A HUNDRED.
I DON'T REALLY LIKE STRAWBERRIES.
She's hardcore.
FOR REAL?!

NO WAY! WHY NOT?!
BUT THEY'RE SO TINY AND DELICIOUS!
NUH-UH!
THEY'RE SOUR.
HOW COULD ANYBODY NOT LIKE STRAW-BERRIES?
Geez.
Is it really that shocking?
...
...
...
GLANCE
..?
What?
SO... IT'D BE OKAY IF THEY WERE SWEET?
YEAH, SWEET IS OKAY.
YOU KNOW... WELL...
AFTER WE GOT HOME, I MADE JAM WITH MY MOM.
IT'S 100% HOME-MADE!
HEH HEH HEH!
YOU JUST KEEP STIRRING AND STIR-RING.
IT'S KINDA...
I MEAN, THE COLOR ISN'T NICE LIKE THE KIND THEY SELL, BUT IT TASTES GOOD!
I WANTED TO GIVE YOU SOME, RITSUKA.
ME?

UH-HUH.
DON'T WORRY. IT'S REALLY SWEET.
YOU WANT SOME ...?

...
SURE.

WHEE!
THEN I'LL BRING IT TO SCHOOL TOMORROW.
Secretly!
COOL.

TO RITSUKA

...

HE SAID HE WANTED IT...
SLUMP

TMP TMP TMP TMP
NO!
STOP IT!!
EWW! WHAT THE HELL IS THIS?!
GIVE IT BACK!

HEY!
YOU CAN'T BRING THIS TO SCHOOL!
STOP IT!
IT LOOKS LIKE POOP. IS IT EVEN EDIBLE?
EWWW!
DUMP IT! IN THE TRASH!
BLEH!
GIVE IT BACK! GIVE IT BACK!
NO!
WHAT IS THIS?
GIVE IT BACK!
TO RITSU
JAM, I GUESS?
IT SAYS, "TO RITSUKA"!!
EWWW!
HA HA HA!
BET YOU'D GET FOOD POISONING FROM THIS.
PFFT
PFFT
WANT A TASTE FIRST?
NO WAY! GROSS!
NO...!!

BRINGING STUFF LIKE THIS TO SCHOOL...
GLOOP
!!
...IS AGAINST THE RULES.
GLOOP GLOOP
TUNK
THERE YOU GO!! ALL GONE!!
ZWAAAAA
NGH...

NGH...
PLIP
PLIP
AH...
AH...
NNGH...
WAAAAH!
OH SHUT UP.
WHAT'RE YOU CRYING FOR? IT'S YOUR FAULT.
IDIOT!
SHE MAKES ME SICK.
LET'S GO.
SNIFF...
SNF...
I...
I MADE IT FOR RITSUKA...
I WENT... TO PICK STRAW-BERRIES...
"WHAT? YOU'RE GIVING IT TO A BOY? GOOD FOR YOU, YUIKO!"
"HEH HEH HEH... THINK HE'LL LIKE IT?"
"OF COURSE HE WILL."
M...
MOMMY...
BWEHH!
HEY, DON'T CRY.

TINK

LICK

YOU'RE RIGHT.

IT'S GOOD.

YOU SHOULD HAVE KNOWN BETTER, YUIKO.
BRINGING SOMETHING LIKE THIS WAS AN INVITATION FOR THEM TO MAKE YOU MISERABLE.

BWAMM

大空
大空

THIS HERE.

WHO DID THIS?

TO RITSUKA

!!
HUH? WHAT IS THAT?
MURMUR
GAR-BAGE?
WHAT'S GOING ON?
THAT WAS REALLY CRUEL.
IT MAKES ME DOUBT YOUR HUMANITY.
MURMUR
MURMUR
WHAT?
WHAT'S HE TALKING ABOUT?
BUT...
...IT'S HER FAULT FOR BRING-ING IT!
HIC
YEAH, THAT'S RIGHT!
HIC
RAR
AND YUIKO BROKE THE RULES!
RAR
IT'S A RULE.
IT'S AGAINST THE RULES!
HMM.
SO IT WAS YOU.
ARE YOU SAYING YOU'VE NEVER BROKEN THE RULES?
THAT'S GOT NOTHING TO DO WITH IT...
IT'S YUIKO'S FAULT!
YIKES
YIKES
YIKES
YUIKO DID SOME-THING WRONG!

WHO GETS HURT BY YUIKO BRINGING THIS TO SCHOOL?

TO RITSUKA

YUIKO DID NOTHING WRONG. SHE DIDN'T HURT ANYBODY.

BUT YOU STILL WENT AND HURT HER.

PEOPLE WHO HURT OTHERS ARE A LOT WORSE...

...THAN PEOPLE WHO BREAK RULES.

I THINK YOU SHOULD ALL DIE!

ERK!
I KNOW HOW YOU FEEL.
BUT BREAKING THE RULES ISN'T RIGHT, EITHER.
RITSUKA.
OOPS.
AND YOU SHOULDN'T SAY THINGS LIKE THAT TO YOUR FRIENDS.
BON-G
BIN-G
GUIDANCE ROOM
SNF
SNF
HIC
HAWATARI, DON'T CRY...
BWUT MIZ ZINO-NOBE...
SNURF
SNIFF
SNUFF

I'M SOOO SORRY!
I OUGHT TO HAVE GONE BY YUIKO'S HOUSE TO PICK IT UP.
SLUURP
RITSUKA.
IT'S AGAINST THE RULES TO STOP ANYWHERE ON THE WAY HOME TOO!
...

MS. SHINO-NOME.
IT'S WAY WORSE TO HURT SOMEONE'S FEELINGS THAN TO HURT THEIR BODY.
THAT'S WHAT I THINK.
RITSUKA ...

SMILE
Moving along!
THANKS FOR THE SNACK!
CHAK
HEY ...
RITSUKA, HOLD ON!
LATER, MS. SHINO-NOME.

PACHAK
AH!
SNIFF
SNIFF
SIGH...
GEEZ...
CAN'T I GET ANYTHING RIGHT?
SNIFF
MS. SHINONOME?
SNIFF
UM.
CAN I TELL YOU SOMETHING?
YES.
HONK
MS. SHINONOME!
I...
I REALLY LIKE RITSUKA.

I THOUGHT HE WAS COOL AND ALL WHEN HE TRANSFERRED HERE.

I WANTED TO BE HIS FRIEND.

BUT NOW, AFTER TODAY, I LIKE HIM EVEN MORE.

RITSUKA'S REALLY NICE TO ME.

I WOULD DO ANYTHING FOR RITSUKA, BUT I DON'T KNOW WHERE TO START.

RITSUKA PROTECTED ME.

I'D DO ANYTHING FOR RITSUKA.

I'D EVEN DIE FOR HIM.

SHE MAY STILL BE TOO YOUNG TO COMPREHEND IT.
YEAH.
I UNDERSTAND.

BUT NO TALKING ABOUT DYING, OKAY?
UNH...
SNIFF SNIFF
SNIFF
'KAY.
TO SAY YOU'RE WILLING TO DIE FOR SOMEONE...

THAT'S LOVELY.

MS. SHINONOME. I HEAR THERE WAS SOME COMMOTION IN YOUR CLASS TODAY.
WAS IT RITSUKA AOYAGI?
AH HA HA.
OH NO, IT WASN'T RITSUKA'S FAULT...
I think.

BUT...

...WHAT SORT OF CHILD IS RITSUKA?

HIS EYES ARE COLD.

HIS SMILE IS FORCED.

AND YET...

...HE'S VERY SENSITIVE TO OTHER PEOPLE'S PAIN.

UH...
IS THERE SOMETHING I SHOULD KNOW ABOUT RITSUKA IN HERE?

WELL, THAT FILE CONTAINS TRANSFER LETTERS AND REPORT CARDS...
...FROM HIS PREVIOUS SCHOOL.
AND HE'S BEEN BADLY HURT HIMSELF.

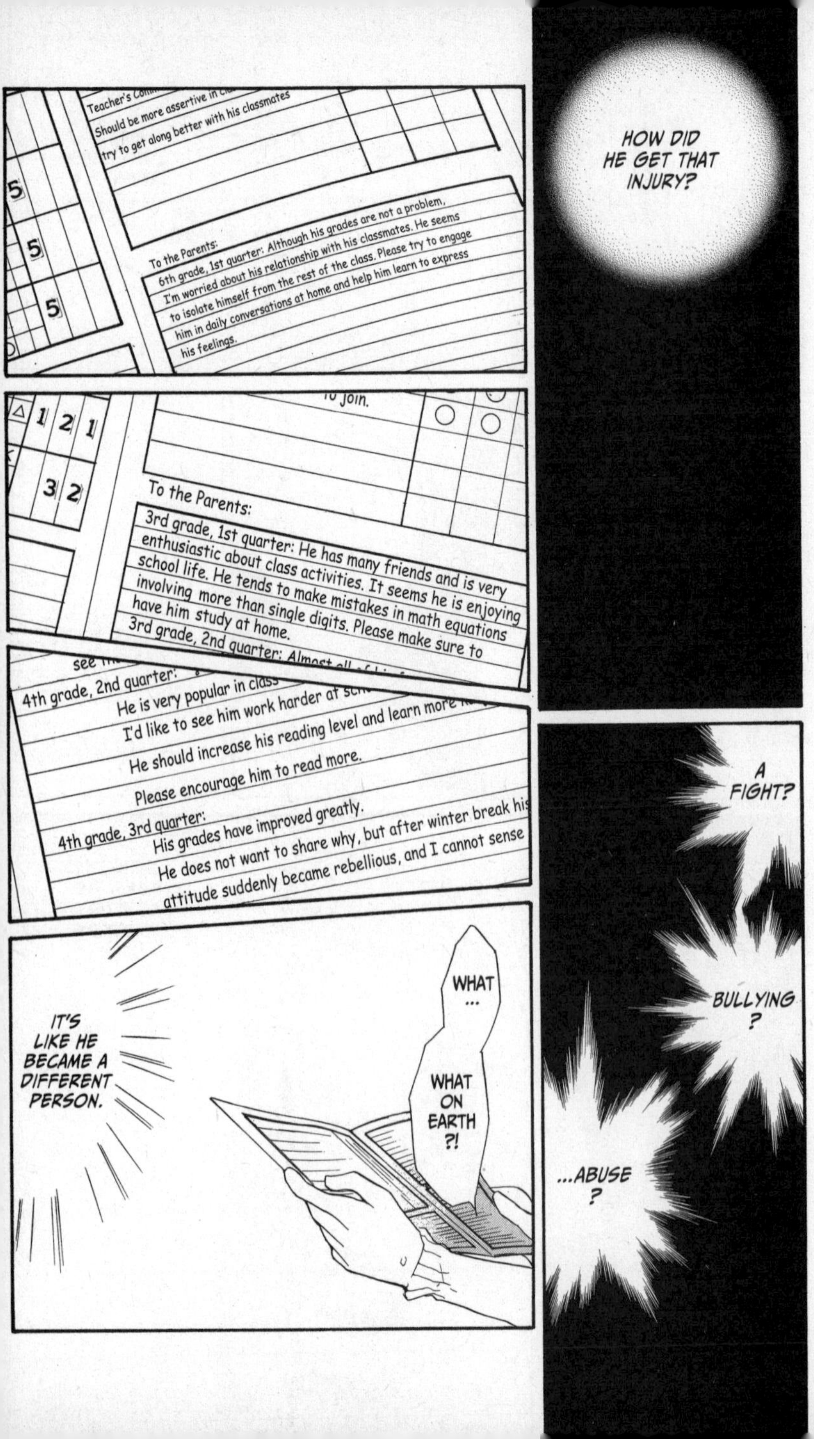

HOW DID HE GET THAT INJURY?

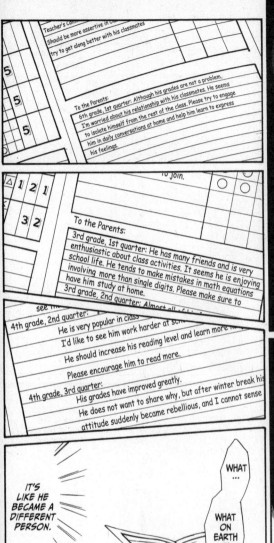

Teacher's Comm...

Should be more assertive in cl...

try to get along better with his classmates

To the Parents:

6th grade, 1st quarter: Although his grades are not a problem, I'm worried about his relationship with his classmates. He seems to isolate himself from the rest of the class. Please try to engage him in daily conversations at home and help him learn to express his feelings.

...to join.

To the Parents:

3rd grade, 1st quarter: He has many friends and is very enthusiastic about class activities. It seems he is enjoying school life. He tends to make mistakes in math equations involving more than single digits. Please make sure to have him study at home.

3rd grade, 2nd quarter: Almost all of his f...

see ...

4th grade, 2nd quarter:

He is very popular in class...

I'd like to see him work harder at sc...

He should increase his reading level and learn more...

Please encourage him to read more.

4th grade, 3rd quarter:

His grades have improved greatly.

He does not want to share why, but after winter break his attitude suddenly became rebellious, and I cannot sense

A FIGHT?
BULLYING?
...ABUSE?

WHAT...

WHAT ON EARTH?!

IT'S LIKE HE BECAME A DIFFERENT PERSON.

WHAT HAPPENED...?

I'd like to see him wor
He should increase his reading level and lea
Please encourage him to read
4th grade, 3rd quarter:
His grades have improved gr
He does not want to share
rebellious, and I
THIS IS WHEN IT STARTED.
BETWEEN THE SECOND AND THIRD QUARTERS OF FOURTH GRADE.
RIGHT ABOUT WHEN RITSUKA TURNED TEN.
WHAT HAPPENED TWO YEARS AGO?
ACCORDING TO THIS, UP UNTIL HE WAS TEN...
...HIS GRADES WEREN'T VERY GOOD, BUT HE WAS HAPPY.
POPULAR WITH HIS CLASSMATES...
LOTS OF FRIENDS...
通知表
AFTER TURNING TEN...
...HE STARTED GETTING TOP GRADES...
BUT BECAME ANTISOCIAL.

CAN PEOPLE CHANGE SO DRASTICALLY? AND IN SUCH A SHORT PERIOD OF TIME?

CAN SOMEONE BECOME A COMPLETELY DIFFERENT PERSON?

DON'T YELL LIKE THAT IN FRONT OF SOME-ONE'S HOUSE.
MY MOM WILL HEAR.
THEN COME TALK WITH US.
No way ...to explain.

HERE.
...
GLARE

HEY! I DIDN'T PUT ANYTHING FUNNY IN IT!
YOU JUST SAW ME BUY IT!!
WHY WOULD YOU BUY ME ANY-THING?
As if.

EXCUSE ME?!
THAT'S SO NOT CUTE!
PLAP
ERK!
!

AI?!
FIGURES ...
YOU'VE GOT A FEVER.
WHAP
LEAVE ME ALONE.
I'M FINE.
ARE THOSE CUTS INFECTED? THEY HURT, RIGHT?

DON'T WORRY ABOUT ME. ANYWAY ...
WHAT DO YOU WANT?
YOU WANNA FIGHT?
HA.
WE WERE TAKEN OFF THE JOB, SO WE AREN'T GOING TO FIGHT YOU ANYMORE.

HUH?

YOU REALLY DON'T KNOW ANYTHING, DO YOU?
OUTSIDE OF THE JOB, WE DON'T HAVE ANYTHING AGAINST YOU.
WE JUST DECIDED TO STOP BY AND SAY HELLO.

WE'RE BEING SENT BACK TO SCHOOL.
AND I DON'T KNOW WHEN WE'LL GET TO LEAVE NEXT.
WE PROBABLY WON'T EVER SEE YOU AGAIN.

NOT LIKE WE WANT TO SEE YOU ANYWAY.
SCHOOL ...?

A SCHOOL FOR FIGHTERS.
SOUBI WENT THERE TOO.

SOUBI ?!

LOOK... DON'T LET HIM FOOL YOU.
HE'S REALLY BAD NEWS.
NOD

I KNOW THAT MUCH.
BUT...
YOU GUYS ARE JUST AS BAD.
WHAT DID YOU DO TO SEIMEI?!
...
RSSH
ANYWAY.
I'M SURE WE'LL BE REPLACED.

THE SCHOOL WILL SEND SOMEONE ELSE.
AND THAT TEAM WILL TAKE YOU DOWN!

AS IF I'D LET THAT HAPPEN!
I'M NOT GOING ANYWHERE!

BECAUSE IF THIS "RITSUKA" DISAPPEARS TOO, WHAT WOULD MOM DO...?

AOYAGI

I'M AT...
...RITSUKA'S HOUSE!!
BDMP
BDMP
BDMP
WHAT SHOULD I DO?
I JUST CAME HERE ON IMPULSE.

A HOUSE CALL? IT'S KINDA SUDDEN.
AWW, NOW WHAT?
SWEAT

HM?

OH MY! CIGARETTE BUTTS?
HMPH!
Not cool!!
NO PUBLIC DECENCY!
OH!!
HE'S...
...MR. AGATSUMA!

MR. AGA-TSUMA ...

OH, CRUD!
BLUUUUSH
YES ...?
EEE!
AND YOU ARE?

WELL ...
I KNOW HIM...
UH.
...BUT HE DOESN'T KNOW ME!
AAUGH!
BLUSH
BLUSH
UM...
BLUSH
I... I...
I'M RITSUKA'S TEACHER ...

I SOUND SO SUSPICIOUS!
WHAT SHOULD I DO?!
I'M A TEACHER AT YANO JONAN ELEMENTARY SCHOOL. MY NAME IS SHINONOME ...

RITSUKA'S TEACHER ...?
AND YOU KNOW ME?

UH... YES.
I SAW YOU AT THE SCHOOL GATE YESTERDAY, AND WHEN I ASKED...
...RITSUKA TOLD ME YOUR NAME.
RITSUKA TALKED ABOUT ME...
SMILE
SKFF
AND SO?
DO YOU HAVE BUSINESS WITH RITSUKA?
IS THIS A HOUSE CALL?
ER...
WELL, UH...
I HAD SOME-THING ON MY MIND... BUT NO BIG...
WHA...
UH...
WHAT'S HIS DEAL?
I... UH...
IS HE REALLY A FRIEND OF RITSUKA'S BROTHER?

HEY, MS. SHINONOME!

HOW OLD ARE YOU?
HUH?
ME...? MY AGE?
BDMP
BDMP
ME?
I'M 23.
BLUSH

23!

YOU'RE PRETTY OLD.

I DON'T REALLY GO FOR OLDER WOMEN.

HEY!
WHY'D YOU SAY THAT?!
I COULD HEAR YOU!!
WHAT ARE YOU SAYING, MR. AGATSUMA?!
BLUSH
THAT'S NEVER GOING TO HAPPEN!!

RIT-SUKA!
RIT-SUKA!

IT'D BE ANNOYING IF SHE GOT A CRUSH ON ME, SO I HAD TO NIP IT IN THE BUD.
WHA...!! EXCUSE ME?!

REALLY?

THEN DON'T CRY.

PLIP PLIP

!!

...

PLIP

ER...

MS. SHINONOME, ARE YOU OKAY?

SOUBI!!
APOLOGIZE TO HER!
YES, SIR!

MS. SHINONOME, I'M VERY SORRY.
SMILE
Agh!

WOBBL
THIS IS...
...HUMILI-ATING!

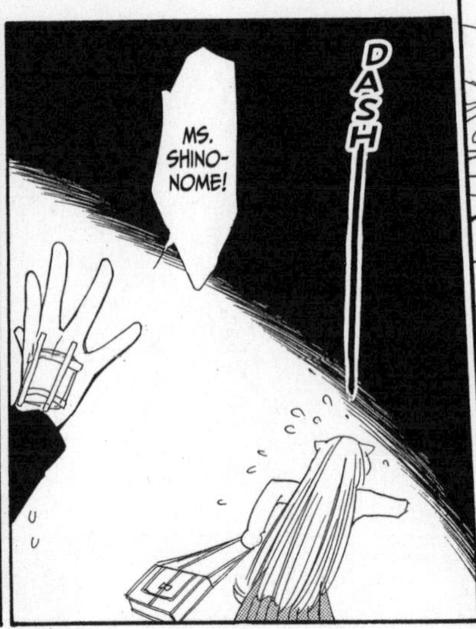
DASH
MS. SHINO-NOME!

...
Ack...
THERE SHE GOES ...

WH... WHAT THE HELL WAS THAT?!
WHY DID YOU MAKE HER CRY?!
RARR
WHY...? I JUST TOLD YOU.

IT WOULD BE INCONVENIENT IF A PERSON LIKE THAT FELL IN LOVE WITH ME.
SOUBI !!

WHAT A MEAN THING TO SAY!
WHY ARE YOU LIKE THAT?
ARE YOU ANGRY ?

THEN...
PUNISH ME.
DO AS YOU SEE FIT, RITSUKA.

GO AHEAD.
ANY WAY YOU LIKE.

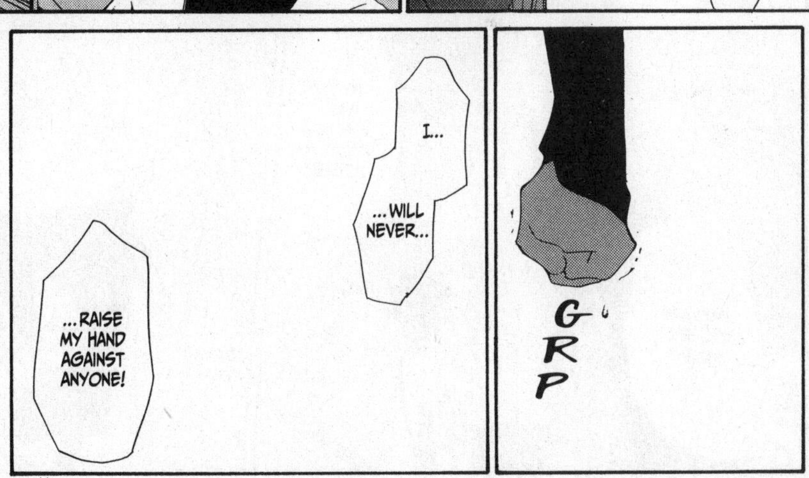
GRP
I...
...WILL NEVER...
...RAISE MY HAND AGAINST ANYONE!

I WILL NEVER USE VIOLENCE.

TOO BAD.
THIS IS MORE DISCIPLINE THAN VIOLENCE, THOUGH.

I SAID NO, AND I MEAN IT!
NO!!
OKAY, OKAY.
GRR
BY THE WAY... WHY WAS SHE AT MY HOUSE?
WHO KNOWS ...?
WHY ARE *YOU* HERE, SOUBI?
Just for a quick stalk.

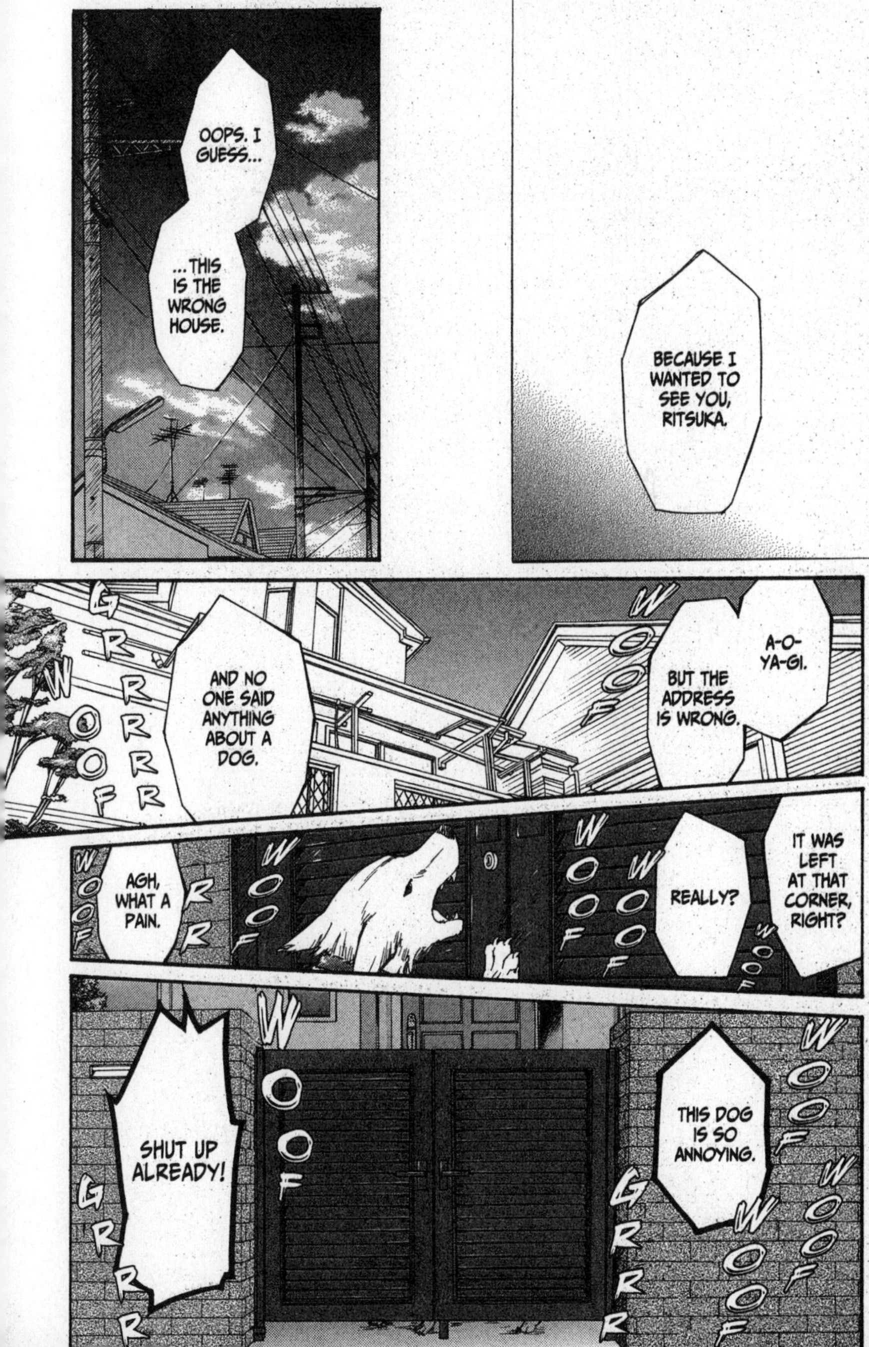

BECAUSE I WANTED TO SEE YOU, RITSUKA.

OOPS. I GUESS...
...THIS IS THE WRONG HOUSE.

A-O-YA-GI.
BUT THE ADDRESS IS WRONG.
WOOF
AND NO ONE SAID ANYTHING ABOUT A DOG.
GRRRRRR
WOROOF
IT WAS LEFT AT THAT CORNER, RIGHT?
WOOF
REALLY?
WOOF
WOOF
WOOF
RRR
AGH, WHAT A PAIN.
WOOF
WOOF
THIS DOG IS SO ANNOYING.
WOOF
GRRRR
WOOF
SHUT UP ALREADY!
GRRRR

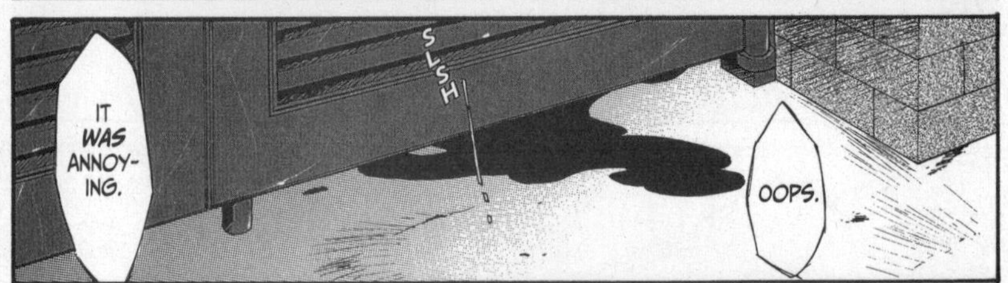

THIS IS SUCH A HASSLE.

SERIOUSLY, MAN.

WHERE ARE YOU, RITSUKA AOYAGI?

I MEAN, DO WE JUST HAVE NO SENSE OF DIRECTION?

TOY'S MASTER / THE ABSOLUTE TOY MASTER CHAPTERS
CHAPTER 2

LET'S SEE.
WHAT'LL IT BE?
SUMMER MANDARIN JELLY?
OR YUBARI MELON CREAM SODA?
UGH.
夏みかんゼリー
Fire

MIDORI...
...YOU REALLY HAVE STRANGE TASTE IN SODA.
WHY DO YOU SAY THAT?
FINE, GET WHATEVER. THE BUS IS COMING.
SIGH
OKAY, OKAY.

BUMMER...
I WON'T BE ABLE TO DRINK THIS ONCE WE'RE BACK AT SCHOOL.
VROOM
FUTAGOTAMA
...
WHO CARES...?
HEY!

HM?
TWITCH
WHAT IS IT, KIN?

AH.
TWITCH

VWEEEN
SOME-ONE'S CLOSE.
THERE'S A FIGHTER OTHER THAN SOUBI NEARBY.
IT'S NOT SOUBI?
NO, IT'S NOT...
THE BATTLE RADIUS IS TOO SMALL FOR IT TO BE SOUBI.
WHO IS IT?
THIS SMELLS FISHY...
THEY'RE HERE ALREADY. THAT WAS QUICK.
VROOM
IT *WAS* QUICK.
BUT TOO BAD.

WE CAN'T DO ANYTHING NOW.
THEY'RE JUST GOING TO HAVE TO DEAL WITH IT ON THEIR OWN.
THAT KID...
...AND SOUBI.
GLUNK
YEAH...
VROOM
FUTAGOTAMA
THEY'RE GONE...
SWISH
OH WELL.
IF THEY DON'T INTEND TO ATTACK, THEN I GUESS IT DOESN'T MATTER.

KIN...

IS THIS SOUBI STRONG?

THAT'S WHAT I HEAR.

I NEVER FOUGHT HIM, SO I DON'T KNOW FOR SURE.

BUT I ASKED THE PRINCIPAL WHAT HE WAS LIKE...

...BECAUSE I HEARD HE WAS A GRADUATE.

MM-HMM.

AND SO?

YOU AND SOUBI, KINKA?

YOU'RE GOING TO FIGHT? THAT'S...

HE TOLD ME SOMETHING REALLY MEAN...

SINCE I HAD THE CHANCE, I ASKED HIM IF SOUBI HAD ANY WEAKNESSES.

SOUBI'S WEAKNESS?

SOUBI HAS NO WEAKNESSES.

HE IS PERFECT.

HE APPARENTLY THOUGHT IT WAS ONLY NATURAL...

...THAT SOUBI WOULD WIN.

GRR GRR

WHAT?!

THE REASON SOUBI FIGHTS AT SUCH A HIGH LEVEL...

...IS BECAUSE HE CAN PICK HIS ATTACKS.

HE CAN CHOOSE TO APPLY PHYSICAL VIOLENCE...

...OR DESTROY THE PSYCHE.

WHAT'S THAT ABOUT?
I DON'T GET IT AT ALL.
BLAH
SOUNDS LAME.
YEAH, DEFINITELY LAME.
BUT WE WON'T KNOW UNTIL WE TRY.
AND I THINK THERE'S AN OPPORTUNITY FOR US TO EXPLOIT RIGHT NOW.
SOUBI WAS PERFECT BECAUSE HE HAD SEIMEI.
BECAUSE HE WAS "BELOVED."
BUT RITSUKA AOYAGI IS NAMED "LOVELESS."
LOVE-LESS?
LIKE, "ONE WITHOUT LOVE"?
AH HA HA...
WHAT A TERRIBLE NAME!

THE SUN'S GOING DOWN.

YOU LIVE IN A NICE AREA.

FLIK

...

...

GO HOME.

BLUSH!!..

I DON'T NEED YOU.

WHY NOT?

I...!!

SOUBI, I DON'T THINK...

...THAT I CAN TRUST YOU.

I WANT TO TRUST YOU...

...BUT I CAN'T!!

WHY'S THAT?

YOU'RE THE ONLY ONE FOR ME, RITSUKA.

YOU CAN'T FOOL ME WITH NICE WORDS.

YOU KNOW THINGS YOU WON'T TELL ME ABOUT.

... ...
DO YOU WANT TO KNOW... RIGHT NOW?
YES, I WANT TO KNOW RIGHT NOW!!
SOUBI...

YOU ALWAYS ASK ME THESE PRYING QUESTIONS...
...BUT NEVER TELL ME ANYTHING ABOUT YOURSELF.
Hands off!
Hey!
THAT'S NOT TRUE AT ALL.
I BELONG TO YOU, RITSUKA.
ALL OF ME.
SHFF

SO I'LL...
...SHOW YOU EVERYTHING. WHAT DO YOU WANT TO SEE?

JOLT

SHAAAA

GOT IT.

I'LL GRANT YOUR WISH RIGHT NOW, RITSUKA.

WHAT ...

TUG

BUT NOT HERE.

COME THIS WAY.

THERE'S AN *ENEMY.*
THEY'RE CLOSE BY. WHAT DO YOU WANT TO DO?

BDMP
AN ENEMY ...
IS IT SEPTIMAL MOON...?

WHOA!
TWITCH
KIN?!
DAMN, HE GOT THE JUMP ON ME.
IT'S SOUBI.
TWK
I DIDN'T EVEN SENSE HIS PRESENCE... DAMMIT!!
EEEN

VWEEE
I...
...RELEASED THE BARRIER. THEY'LL BE HERE SOON.
THE ENEMY.

"ENEMY"...
SO IT'S SEPTIMAL MOON? THE ONES WHO KILLED SEIMEI?!
SWSH

GINKA.
OVER HERE.
ROGER.
RIGHT.
HOW DO YOU WANT ME TO HANDLE THEM, RITSUKA? WANT TO KILL THEM?

WE'VE FOUND YOU, SOUBI!!
AND RITSUKA AOYAGI!!
RSSSH

LET'S FIGHT!
SWSH
I ACCEPT.

HOW DO YOU WANT ME TO HANDLE THEM, RITSUKA?
THAT'S NOT IT.
BDMP
BDMP
I...
DO YOU WANT TO KILL THEM?
HERE.
FWIP
INSIDE THIS ENVELOPE IS THE INFORMATION YOU WANT, RITSUKA.

I WANT TO KNOW THE TRUTH.
IF YOU WIN, IT'S YOURS.
SYSTEMS ...
...EXPAND!

EXPAND.

SWSH

WE WILL BE ON AUTOMATIC.

SOUBI. THEIR ...

SKWEEZ

THE GIRL IS THE SACRIFICE.

I'M UP AGAINST A GIRL.

HA! DON'T WORRY.

I'VE NEVER HAD A MARK LEFT ON ME.

OH MY.

THEN I'LL TRY TO SPARE YOUR FACE.

RIP

BUT I APOLOGIZE IF MY AIM GOES ASTRAY.
HMPH
LIGHTNING.
LIKE TEN MILLION ARROWS.
STRIKE WITH THE SPEED OF THE WIND!
GRAAA

KIN!
RESPOND.
RESPOND ...
THOK
WAH!
THOK
THOK
THOK
HE'S FAST.
THERE'S ONLY A SPLIT SECOND DELAY BETWEEN THE CASTING AND DEPLOYMENT OF THE SPELL.
DRIP
I MADE SURE NOT TO STRIKE YOUR FACE.

NOW IT'S OUR TURN.
USE A FULL POWER ATTACK.
IF IT'S BETWEEN ME AND THAT LITTLE KID, I CAN TAKE WAY MORE PAIN.
WE JUST NEED TO CRUSH THE BRAT.
HE HASN'T GOTTEN SERIOUS YET...
SHOULDN'T WE BE ON DEFENSE?
EVEN IF SOUBI CAN HANDLE IT...
...THERE'S NO WAY THE KID CAN!
SKWEEZ
RITSUKA.
COMMAND ME!!

I...
I WANT THAT ENVELOPE!
GRRK
LICK
...
Um. Was that wrong?
I WANT TO FIND OUT WHY SEIMEI WAS KILLED.
DEFEAT THEM!!
OUR NAME...
...IS SLEEP-LESS.
TWO BEINGS WITH ONE NAME.
VWEE

WITNESS...

...THE DARKNESS...

...OF A SLEEPLESS NIGHT!

FWAAA

GRO

HA

GROO
WE DID IT!
HA HA!
WE RE-STRICTED HIM.
GRRT

RITSUKA.
ARE YOU ALL RIGHT ...?
What is this?
I feel sick.
I'M FINE...
PAT
...
IT'S ONLY ...
...A SHALLOW DARKNESS.
TWITCH
INTERCEDE.
INTERFERE.
COME, STARS!!

SOUBI'S VOICE...

CUT OPEN THE DARKNESS AND FILL THE SKY WITH STARS.

PIXELS OF SPARKLING LIGHT...

...DEFY...

...THE NIGHT.

HIS VOICE IS COMFORTING.

THE STARS ARE FIRM IN THE FIRMAMENT.

LIGHT...

...ENTERS.

IT INVADES.

SOMETHING HURTS... AM I LOSING BLOOD? SUFFOCATING?

ZUWAAA
HIS WARM, DRY HANDS...
KIN! TURN OFF THE STARS.
I WANT BLACK CLOUDS.
IT FEELS NICE WHEN SOUBI TOUCHES ME.

THICK, DARK CLOUDS.
BLACK CLOUDS BLOCK ALL LIGHT.
WOOOOOOM
ERASE THE STARS AND TRAP OUR ENEMY ...
...IN JET BLACK ...
DEEP, DARK CLOUDS FULL OF...
...LIGHTNING AND ELECTRICITY.
BECOME A VICIOUS THUNDERSTORM...

...AND PUNCTURE THE DARKNESS.
COME, DARK-NESS.
HE'S NOT JUST FAST...
CONCEAL EVERYTHING!
HE'S USING OUR OWN SPELLS AGAINST US!

PENE-
TRATE.
COME, LIGHT.
PENE-TRATE EVERY-THING
!!
NOT ONE WORD ...
...OF DEFENSE ?
NGH...!
SHAA
VWOO

BSHANG
THIS IS BAD.
THE MO-MENTUM'S IN THEIR FAVOR.
DEFEND ...
ISN'T SOUBI HURTING TOO...?
SHIELD US...
...FROM THE ENEMY'S EYES...
VWOOO
JANGLE
OH... HE'S BLEED-ING!!
...IN A PITCH BLACK ...
... CURTAIN OF DARK-NESS.
FLAMES.

ENVELOP THEM WITH SCORCHING PAIN.

BURN BRIGHT, HELLFIRE.

FOOOOM

SLICE THROUGH THE DARKNESS.

TEAR EVERYTHING ASUNDER!

FOOOM

!!

HGCK!

WHATEVER PAIN I'M FEELING...

...I'M SURE THAT SOUBI IS SUFFERING MORE.

YOUR METHODS ARE WRONG!
YOU PISS ME OFF!
ALL YOU'RE DOING IS COASTING ON THE BACKS OF OUR SPELLS!
IF YOU BRING DARKNESS, I BRING STARS.
IF YOU BRING CLOUDS, I BRING RAIN.
IF YOU BRING A SHROUD, I BRING A FUNERAL PYRE.
TO TURN AN OPPONENT'S POWER BACK AGAINST THEM...
THAT'S ELEMENTARY.
OOH, THE MODEL STUDENT!
I'M SICK OF YOU!
I CAN SEE WHY YOU WERE THE PRINCIPAL'S PET. YOU PLAY DIRTY.
TWITCH
HE REACTED?! BUT TO WHAT?
TO "PRINCIPAL"?
TO "PET"?
TO "MODEL STUDENT"?
TO "DIRTY"?
TO WHAT?

EVERY-ONE...
...RE-CEIVED THE SAME INSTRUC-TION.
SO IT'S TO "PET"?!
HE ONLY PRAISED ME OUT OF NAR-CISSISM.
NO, IT WAS TO "PRINCI-PAL."
THE PRINCI-PAL...
HE TAUGHT ME YOUR WEAKNESS.

WHO'D HAVE THOUGHT SAYING THAT WOULD PROVIDE AN OPENING?!
RE-STRICT!!
YOU CAN NO LONGER MOVE!

SHAANK
!!
JANGLE.
THAT'S RATHER...
...UN-PLEASANT.
BLACKNESS CRUSHES YOUR BODY AND SOUL.
DENY FREEDOM!
RE-STRICT!
RE-STRICT!
HAA
SKW
NGH...
I'M SORRY. ARE YOU IN PAIN ...?
YOUR HEART'S BEATING SO FAST.
SOUBI.
YOU CAN DO IT...

I WANT THAT ENVELOPE NO MATTER WHAT.

LICK

TWK

GO GET IT!!

DON'T LOSE...

TOY'S MASTER / THE ABSOLUTE TOY MASTER CHAPTERS

CHAPTER 3

THE ENEMY'S NAME IS SLEEPLESS.
A NIGHT WITHOUT SLEEP.
WE DID IT!!
WE'VE RESTRICTED THEM!!
THIS IS LAUGHABLE.
HOW PATHETIC.
I SEE THROUGH YOUR SLEEPLESS NIGHT.

THAT ENVE-LOPE.
GO GET IT!
ABSOLUTE.
YES...
...MASTER.
KIN! IT'S OUR TURN.
WHEN HE GOES TO REMOVE THE BONDS, THAT'S OUR CHANCE TO STRIKE.
GOT IT.
SHAA
I WON'T REMOVE THEM.
THERE'S NO NEED.
I SHALL ATTACK.

THAT WITHOUT EQUAL.
THAT WHICH OPPRESSES EVERY-THING.
I CAN'T MOVE. IS THIS WHAT "RESTRICTION" MEANS?
GRRK!
OR...
I SHALL ATTACK WITH ABSOLUTE POWER.
FLAMES.
ROARING FLAMES.
...IS IT JUST...
...SOUBI'S STRONG ARMS AROUND ME?

RAZE!!
VWOO
GYAAH!!
EEE!
BWASH
BACHANG

PCHIING

WH
YOU BASTARD!
AM

I CAN'T STAND YOU!!
WHA...

WHAT ARE YOU DOING?!
BACK OFF!
TSH

WHUMP
Ack!
SHOOF
IF YOU WANT TO SLUG IT OUT ...
...I'M FINE WITH THAT TOO.
OOF.
FWUMP
KIN!
HOLD ON!
NO FIGHT LEFT?
YANK
EEEEP! EEEP!
ENOUGH ALREADY, SOUBI!

HERE.

...UH...

WHAT WILL I...

...FIND INSIDE?

FREEDOM.

THAT'S WHAT YOU HAVE THERE, RITSUKA.

CHOICE.
THAT'S WHAT...
...YOU MUST MAKE, RITSUKA.
THE LAWS OF THE WORLD...
...HAVE DISINTE-GRATED BETWEEN YOU AND ME.
YOU ARE MY LAW, RITSUKA.
MY REASON FOR LIVING...
...IS YOU ALONE.
I AM YOUR FIGHTER.
USE ME AS YOU SEE FIT.
COMMAND ME.
DO IT AS YOU WISH.
WE ARE...

HE...
...WHO IS TO BE COM-MANDED.

AND HE WHO COM-MANDS.
...

IS THAT ALL WE ARE?
NEVER MIND.

RITSUKA?
TWIRL
IT'S NOTH-ING.

ARE YOU ANGRY, RITSUKA?
I'M NOT MAD!
WHO SAYS I'M MAD?!
RIP

W098N074A11T0005

DOOM
WHAT ...?
THIS IS IT?
WHAT THE...
WHAT DOES THIS HAVE TO DO WITH SEIMEI?
A74O
LETTERS AND NUMBERS... I GUESS.
MAYBE A CODE?
HISS HISS
HISS
AW, MAAAN!
SIGH
...
...
OKAY...

W098N074A11T0005

ABOUT THIS NOTE.

IF YOU CAN REMEMBER ANYTHING, TELL ME IMMEDIATELY.

YES, SIR.

dead serious

WHAT IS IT? I HAVE NO IDEA.

AN EN-CRYPTED CODE? A SERIAL NUMBER?

AN ID NUMBER? A PASS-WORD?

FOR WHAT? TO WHERE?

MAYBE IF... IT WAS SOME KIND OF WORD OR HIDDEN MEANING...

SWF
YOU GOT A SCRAPE.
I THINK YOU'D BETTER TREAT THIS.
KT
UNK
WHAT ARE YOU DOING ...?
not so serious

OH.
I'M SORRY. IT'S MORE IMPORTANT ...
KLAK
KLAK
...THAT I TAKE CARE OF YOU, SOUBI!
BUT I'M FINE.
NO, YOU'RE NOT. I'M GOING TO TREAT THAT CUT.

WHY IS THIS ...
...BLEED-ING?
BECAUSE I'M GOING AGAINST MY NAME.
OH...
UH...

COME TO THINK OF IT ...
THAT GUY MENTIONED A PRINCIPAL.

HEY...
HUH?
I DON'T WANT TO TALK ABOUT IT.
HMPH!
I DON'T WANT TO SPEAK OF IT.

SUDDENLY I REALIZED...

INSTEAD OF BEING TOLD TO "COMMAND HIM" OR HEARING THAT HE WOULD "DO ANYTHING I SAY"...

...THIS MADE ME HAPPIER.
AFTER ALL...
...I...
I WANT SOMETHING REAL.
THEN...
...DO AS YOU PLEASE.

THERE'S NO NOW OR LATER.
IT'S OKAY. I WON'T ASK RIGHT NOW.

WHA— WHY ?!
That's an order!
D-DUM
EVEN IF YOU COMMAND ME, I WON'T DO IT.
I wanna know!
WHY NOT ?!
That's not the deal!

WELL FINE, THEN! GO HOME!
WHAP
THIS CODE IS YOUR HOMEWORK!! THINK ABOUT IT LONG AND HARD!

YOU'RE SO FEISTY, RITSUKA.
4A11T0005

Bah!
GOOD NIGHT.
SWSSH
RSSH
RSSH
KIN... LET'S GO HOME.
WOBL...
NGH...
OH! LOOKS LIKE YOU FAILED AFTER ALL.

SHA

YO!!

SHASHASHA

!!

IT'S YOU!!

WHAT'S ...

...WITH THAT BLOOD?

YOU DID SOMETHING BAD AGAIN...

URRK!

SIGH
BLUB

STARE
PLIP

I'm...
...tired.
BLUB
POKE

SSH
BEEP BEEP BEEP
SSH
K-TOMP
AN EMAIL ?!
0928soubi@docomo.ne.jp
I forgot.
BDMP BDMP
BDMP BDMP
BIP BIP
e.jp
I forgot.
To Ritsuka
BADUMP
I forgot.
To Ritsuka
Kiss me.

"I FORGOT."

SHAKE

"RITSUKA."

"KISS ME."

SHAKE SHAKE

HUH?!

K...

KISS ?!

PEEK PEEK

WHAT'S IT MEAN? WHAT AM I SUPPOSED TO DO?

SPLISH

...

Inbox 1

0928soubi@docomo.ne.jp

I forgot.

To Ritsuka

Kiss me.

IS HE SOME KIND OF IDIOT...?

PLIP...

KISS

HEY, I WENT OUT SHOPPING.
GOT A MIDNIGHT SNACK.
FUMP

THANKS.
IT'S GONNA BE AN ALL-NIGHTER.
OKAY.
IF YOU DON'T HURRY YOU WON'T MAKE IT TO THE EXHIBITION.
HERE'S THAT RICE BALL BENTO YOU ORDERED.
YOU DON'T USUALLY EAT THIS STUFF.

I'M CURIOUS HOW THEY TASTE.
HUH.
IT ACTUALLY LOOKS PRETTY GOOD.
IT'S THE BEST!
HEY, SOU...
... YOU'VE ... CHANGED, HAVEN'T YOU?
YOU THINK?
PWEEP
UH-HUH. FOR SURE!
PWEEP
PWEEP
BECAUSE OF THAT KID OR SOMETHING.
OH, AN EMAIL.
SOU !!
THIS IS A SERIOUS CONVER-SATION HERE!
!
AGH!
ERK!
HEH HEH
WHAT THE HELL?
YOU PERV!

YUP.
I'M GETTING HARD.

WHAT, WHAT?! GROSS!
A SEXY EMAIL?! FROM WHO?
LET ME SEE! SHOW ME!!
CHAK
You freak-show!
What are you saying?
I can't stand this anymore!
NOPE.

WHY, YOU!
HEY!
BAM
BAM
BAM
HEY!!

HEE!

Hurry up and go to sleep!

Mwa

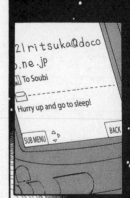

* Please, please Don't cry like that I'm going to go crazy I don't want to see you Seeing you again It makes me sick Because the instant we have to say goodbye I want to die

* Once I desire something I can't restrain myself Restraint
It's impossible for me I desire it Until it becomes mine
But there is no end No matter how much I take for myself

LOVELESS YUNKOUGA NO.04
TOY'S MASTER /
THE ABSOLUTE TOY MASTER
CHAPTERS
CHAPTER 4

What a lame conversation.

RITSUKA, WANT TO JOIN THE ARTS AND CRAFTS CLUB?

ARTS AND CRAFTS...? DUNNO ABOUT THAT...
I MEAN, I CAN'T REALLY DRAW AND ALL.
ERGH
IT'S NOT REALLY ABOUT DRAWING.
ACTUALLY I'M JUST NOT VERY GOOD WITH MY HANDS.

THEN HOW ABOUT THE ORCHESTRA ?!
KA
CHAK
RIGHT NOW WE'RE LOOKING FOR ACCORDION PLAYERS!!
LIKE I SAID...
...I DON'T WANT ANYTHING TOO INVOLVED.
OOH, THE ORCHESTRA! THAT SOUNDS FUN! ♡
NOBODY KNOWS HOW TO PLAY WHEN THEY START!!
THEN HOW ABOUT THE ENGLISH CLUB?
I'M THEIR FACULTY ADVISOR, YOU KNOW.
UH.
BUT MS. SHINONOME, THE ENGLISH CLUB IS ALL GIRLS, ISN'T IT?!
WHAT'S WRONG WITH THAT? IT'S EXTRA FUN WITH SO MANY GIRLS.
THE ARTS AND CRAFTS CLUB IS ALL GIRLS TOO.
NO, I WANT RITSUKA TO...
ANYWAY...

WEDNESDAYS ...

...AREN'T GOOD FOR ME.

"I HAVE TO GO TO THE HOSPITAL EVERY WEEK."

I'VE ALWAYS SAID IT LIKE THAT, AND THEN KEPT MY DISTANCE FROM EVERYONE.

BUT TODAY THOSE WORDS WOULDN'T COME OUT.

THAT HAS NEVER...
I really...
...hate this.
...HAPPENED BEFORE.
HOW ARE YOU, RITSUKA?
IT'S BEEN A WEEK.
DOING WELL?
FINE, I GUESS.
DID ANYTHING INTERESTING HAPPEN THIS WEEK?
ALWAYS THE SAME CONVERSATION.
NOT REALLY...
Y'KNOW, TODAY...
...INSTEAD OF ANSWERING MY QUESTIONS, WHY DON'T YOU JUST TALK, RITSUKA?

HUH...?

I'D LIKE TO HEAR WHAT YOU HAVE TO SAY.
YOU SEEM LIKE YOU'RE IN A GOOD MOOD TODAY.
THE SUBJECT DOESN'T MATTER, JUST TALK ABOUT ANYTHING.

THEN...
DR. KATSUKO...
HM?
ARE YOU A PICKY EATER?

"RITSUKA" ALWAYS ATE A LOT OF JUNK.

AND MOM IS HUNG UP ON THAT, SO I CAN'T ASK HER TO CHANGE IT.

I MEAN, IT DOESN'T REALLY MATTER TO ME EITHER WAY.

BUT LATELY...

...I'VE BEEN TRYING MORE THINGS.

I ATE FERMENTED SOYBEANS.

AND TOFU AND ASPARAGUS.

AND I THOUGHT THEY WERE REALLY GOOD.

IT SURPRISED ME.

HOW LOVELY!

WHO DID YOU EAT WITH?

STARE
WITH...
WITH A FRIEND...
RITSUKA.
YOU ARE A NORMAL PERSON.
AND YOU'RE A WONDERFUL BOY.
SMILE
YOUR MOTHER, AND MAYBE EVEN YOU, YOURSELF, CAN'T QUITE ACCEPT THIS...
BUT I KNOW.

I LIKE YOU A LOT, RITSUKA.
...
YOU LIKE ...
...ME ?
I DON'T KNOW WHY. I SHOULD BE HAPPY.
BUT I DON'T LIKE TO BE TOLD THAT.
I'M SORRY.
DR. KATSUKO.
WHY IS THAT?
SOMEONE SAYS "I LIKE YOU," (NOT THAT I HEAR IT OFTEN)...
...AND MY HEART GOES COLD.

WHETHER A CLASSMATE SAYS IT TO ME...
OR THE LUNCH LADY SAYS IT TO ME...
I ALWAYS THINK TO MYSELF...
"WHAT ON EARTH DO THEY MEAN?"

I LOVE YOU.
RITSUKA.
WHEN SOUBI SAYS THAT TO ME...
...IT ONLY HURTS.
SOUBI.

DR. KATSUKO...
I...
I THINK ABOUT LIFE A LOT.
I ALWAYS THINK...
..."IF ONLY MY LIFE COULD GO BACK TO THE WAY IT WAS."
IF ONLY SEIMEI DIDN'T DIE.
IF ONLY RITSUKA HADN'T DISAPPEARED.
THAT'S REALLY WHAT I THINK ABOUT.
I KNOW THAT I CAN'T DO ANYTHING ABOUT SEIMEI.
BUT IF ONLY THE REST WOULD GO BACK TO THE WAY IT WAS.
I DON'T WANT TO MOVE ON.
MEMORIES AND THE PAST, THAT'S WHAT MATTERS.
I DON'T WANT TO GO INTO THE FUTURE.
SKWEEZ
THAT'S WHY IT'S MEANING-LESS FOR ME TO BE HERE RIGHT NOW.

WHEN EVERYTHING GOES BACK TO THE WAY IT WAS...
...I'LL PROBABLY DISAPPEAR.
IT'S MEANING-LESS FOR ME TO BE HERE, BECAUSE I'M ONLY GOING TO DISAPPEAR.
BUT LIFE...
...IS ABOUT TRYING HARD UP UNTIL YOU DISAP-PEAR.
DON'T YOU THINK SO?
YOU'RE NOT THE ONLY ONE WHO IS GOING TO EVENTUALLY DISAPPEAR, RITSUKA.
ONE DAY, EVERYONE DISAPPEARS.

THEN...
WHY WERE WE BORN?
WHY DO WE LIVE?
WHY DO WE DIE?
MAYBE NOBODY KNOWS?
THAT'S RIGHT.
THAT'S NOT FAIR.
I THOUGHT THAT ADULTS WOULD KNOW.

GOOD WORK. I'LL SEE YOU NEXT WEEK.
CHAK
THANK YOU VERY MUCH.
HEY... RITSUKA?
THAT SCRAPE. YOUR MOTHER REALLY DIDN'T DO THAT?
I'M WORRIED ABOUT YOU...
I'LL SEE YOU...
...NEXT WEEK!!
WHAP

WHY ARE YOU IN SUCH A BAD MOOD...
...DR. KATSUKO?
IT'S NOTHING.
I JUST CAN'T FIGURE OUT WHAT HIS MOTHER WANTS.
WHAT DOES SHE WANT FROM RITSUKA?!
SIGH
YOU SHOULDN'T GET SO PERSONALLY INVOLVED.
ERK...!
BUT...!
RITSUKA IS REALLY...
IF I WERE 20 YEARS YOUNGER I'D MAKE A MOVE ON HIM.
OH STOP THAT, DOCTOR.
DR. KATSUKO, YOU HAVE A GUEST.

ME?
I DON'T HAVE ANY APPOINTMENTS SCHEDULED.
IT'S THE POLICE.
THE POLICE...
UH...
IT'S ABOUT RITSUKA AOYAGI...
HMM...
MAME DAIFUKU
THEN, I'LL ALSO TAKE...
...THREE CHESTNUT KANOKO.
KOUYO SHIGURE
Thank you very much!
URH...
KINAKO MOCHI
TAK
TAK
MAYBE I...
...SHOULDN'T HAVE BROUGHT A GIFT AFTER ALL.

I CAN'T REALLY BELIEVE...
BDMP
...I'M GOING ALL THE WAY TO A STUDENT'S HOUSE.
BDMP
IT'S MY FIRST TIME, SO I'M NERVOUS...
BDMP

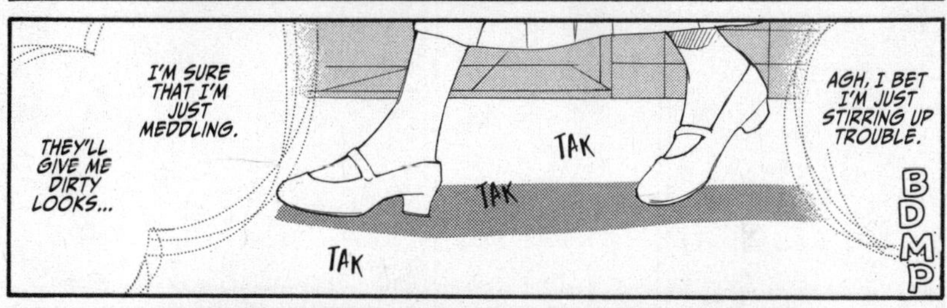
AGH, I BET I'M JUST STIRRING UP TROUBLE.
BDMP
TAK
TAK
TAK
I'M SURE THAT I'M JUST MEDDLING.
THEY'LL GIVE ME DIRTY LOOKS...

BUT I HAVE TO GO!
I CAN'T DO THIS OVER THE PHONE!

AFTER ALL...
THIS IS FOR RITSUKA'S SAKE.
GRIT
I HAVE TO BE ABLE TO DO SOMETHING FOR HIM!

HEY, LADY.
ARE YOU FROM AROUND HERE?
DO YOU KNOW WHERE THE AOYAGI HOUSE IS?

KRCH
WELL?
HUH... AH...
WHEN YOU SAY AOYAGI, DO YOU MEAN...
RITSUKA AOYAGI'S HOUSE.
YOU'RE LOOKING FOR RITSUKA'S HOUSE?
ARE YOU HIS FRIENDS?

FRIENDS?
HEH
HEH
HEH

WELL, THEN.
LET'S GO, LET'S GO.
IF YOU KNOW, THEN SHOW US THE WAY.
OKAY ...
WHAT'S GOING ON? ARE THEY FROM HIS OLD SCHOOL?
HEH
YOU HAVE YOUR EARS.
HEH
HEY LADY, ARE YOU A VIRGIN?
EVEN THOUGH YOU'RE AN ADULT?
THAT'S SO WEIRD!
BLUSH
IT...
IT ISN'T WEIRD.
I LIKE IT THIS WAY!
THAT'S JUST ME, GOING AT MY OWN PACE!

OH REALLY.

BUT NORMALLY...

HEH

...BY THE TIME SOMEONE'S AN ADULT THEY'VE ALREADY HAD SEX...

...AND LOST THEIR EARS.

HEH

Y'KNOW?

THAT MAY BE TRUE!

BUT EVERY-ONE HAS TO DO WHAT'S RIGHT FOR THEM.

I THINK THAT I'M FINE THE WAY I AM!

OH REALLY...?

HEH

YOU'RE...

HEH

HEH

...PRETTY FUNNY.

YUP.

YOU SURE ARE FUNNY.

FUNNY...
YOU THINK SO?
WELL, I THINK YOU TWO...
...ARE VERY CUTE.
WHA...
WHAT THE?!
HA!
CUTE, SHE SAYS!!
HEE
HEE
HEE
HEH
I...
HEH
HEH
I LIKE HER.
YEAH, I LIKE HER TOO.
I...
...DON'T GO FOR OLDER WOMEN.

BLUSH
GOSH.
THE LAST TIME I CAME, MR. AGATSUMA WAS HERE...
HEY!! HE'S YOUNGER THAN ME.
WHY AM I BOTHERING WITH THE "MR."?!
I'M OLDER THAN HIM! BUT HE PROBABLY THINKS I'M SOME OLD MAID!
WHY DID I REMEMBER THAT, OF ALL THINGS?!
THE NEXT TIME I SEE HIM...
...I'LL DROP THE "MR."!
THAT STUPID AGATSUMA!!
GRIND GRIND
GRIND GRIND
HEY...
TELL US YOUR NAME.

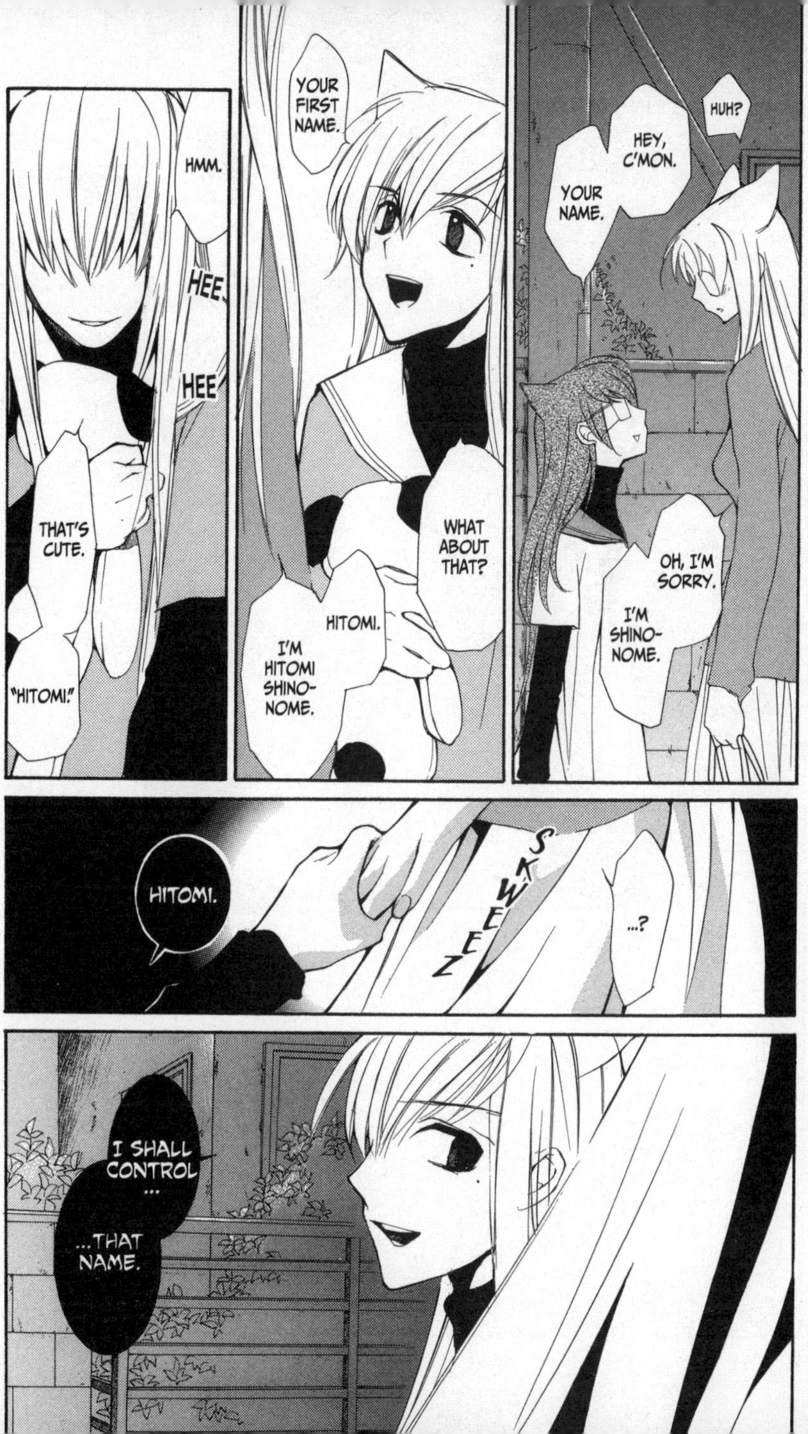

HEY, C'MON.
YOUR NAME.
HUH?
OH, I'M SORRY.
I'M SHINO-NOME.
YOUR FIRST NAME.
WHAT ABOUT THAT?
HITOMI.
I'M HITOMI SHINO-NOME.
HMM.
HEE HEE
THAT'S CUTE.
"HITOMI."

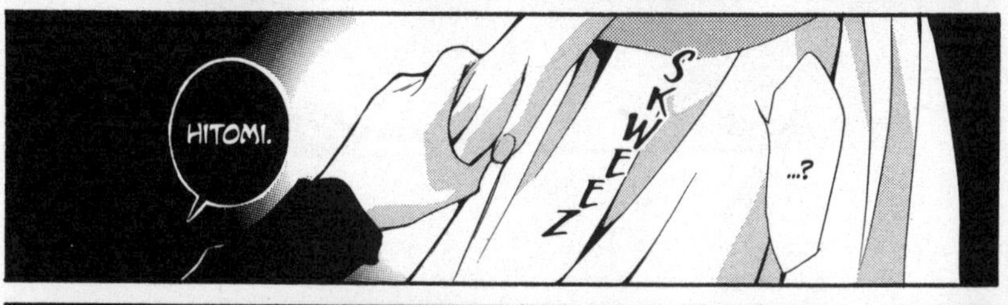
...?
SKWEEZ
HITOMI.

I SHALL CONTROL...
...THAT NAME.

PTCH
MY LEGS...
...WON'T MOVE?
?!
ENSLAVE.
WE HAVE CAPTURED HITOMI.
SHE IS OUR PREY.
DSHAAAA
HITOMI IS OURS.
ALL RIGHT.
HITOMI.
Y'SEE, WE WERE THINKING ...
...THAT IT WAS ABOUT TIME WE GOT RID OF OUR EARS.

TOY'S MASTER / THE ABSOLUTE TOY MASTER CHAPTERS

CHAPTER 5

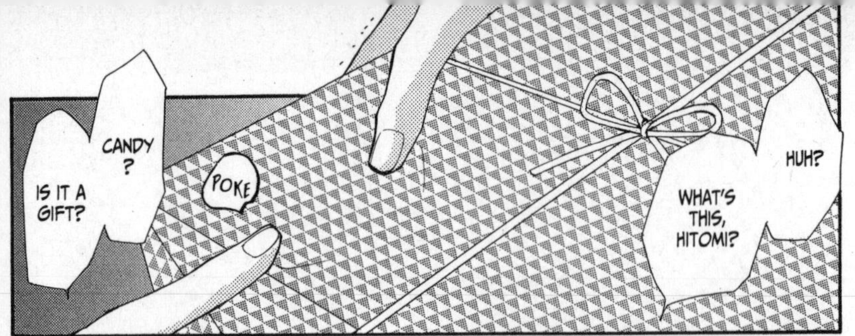

WERE YOU GOING SOMEWHERE?

WHERE?

I WONDER IF THERE'S A GOOD PLACE FOR IT AROUND HERE?

I DUNNO...

Hmm...

YOU AREN'T GETTING AWAY.
... NO...
COME ON.
WHAT...
...DID YOU DO TO ME...

WHERE SHOULD WE GO?
I SAW ONE WHEN WE GOT HERE.
THE PARK. IT'S GOTTA BE THE PARK.
LET'S GO. LET'S GO.

COME ON, WALK WITH YOUR OWN TWO FEET...
HITOMI.
COME ON.

THAT...
THAT'S NOT HOW...
STOMP
...YOU TALK TO YOUR ELDERS.
STOMP
WOW, YOU REALLY DON'T KNOW THE POSITION YOU'RE IN, HITOMI.
CALL ME MS. SHINONOME! WE'VE ONLY JUST MET!
G
RA

I...
...DON'T KNOW...
...WHAT YOU DID TO ME.
BUT I KNOW IT'S NOT FAIR.
FAIR?
WE DON'T LIKE FAIR.
THERE'S NO SUCH THING AS FAIR.

SCRCH

IF I PRETEND I DIDN'T SEE AND JUST WALK AWAY, AND RITSUKA FINDS OUT LATER...

...HE'LL PROBABLY GET REALLY MAD.

I'M LOVELESS'S FIGHTER.
SOUBI AGATSUMA.
MS. SHINO-NOME.
POKE
SWF
TWITCH
GO HOME.
Yeek!
DON'T BUTT IN, SOUBI AGAT-SUMA.
I'M AFRAID I WILL.
WHERE WERE YOU TAKING THIS WOMAN-CHILD?

BLUSH

IF I LEAVE YOU WITH THEM, RITSUKA WILL GET ANGRY.

UH.

MR. AGA...

I MEAN, AGATSUMA.

HUH?! WAIT A MINUTE.

DID HE JUST...

...CALL ME A WOMAN-CHILD?

YOU... YOU...
ARE YOU ALL RITSUKA'S FRIENDS?

HUH?!

I MEAN...
BLUSH
NO!
THAT'S NOT WHAT I MEANT TO SAY.

THIS IS NONE OF YOUR BUSINESS.
SLEEP.
THIS IS NONE OF YOUR BUSINESS.
WHAT A...
...MEAN THING TO SAY!
MR. AGAT-SUMA ...
WHY DO YOU ALWAYS ...
...SAY SUCH TERRIBLE THINGS...
DO I REALLY ...
...SAY SUCH TERRIBLE THINGS?
SLUMP
YOU DO...
THEN I'M SORRY.

GRR GRR GRR GRR GRR GRR

YOU TWO KNOW EACH OTHER?

SHE BE-LONGS TO US.

YOU'RE PISSING US OFF.

GRR GRR GRR GRR GRR

GIVE HER BACK.

I THINK NOT.

IF YOU DON'T, WE'LL KILL YOU.

GRR GRR GRR

THAT'S A REAL THREAT. WE'RE STRONG.

GRR

WE'VE NEVER LOST TO ANYONE.

YOU DON'T EVEN KNOW OUR NAME, DO YOU?

ENOUGH TALK. SHOW ME WHAT YOU'VE GOT.

YOU'RE GONNA REGRET THAT.
WE'RE ...
...ZERO.
ZERO?!
THEY'RE ZEROES ?!
DOMAIN SYSTEMS ...
EXPAND.
VWEEEN
WE DECLARE BATTLE.
SYSTEMS EXPAND.
VWEE
I ACCEPT.

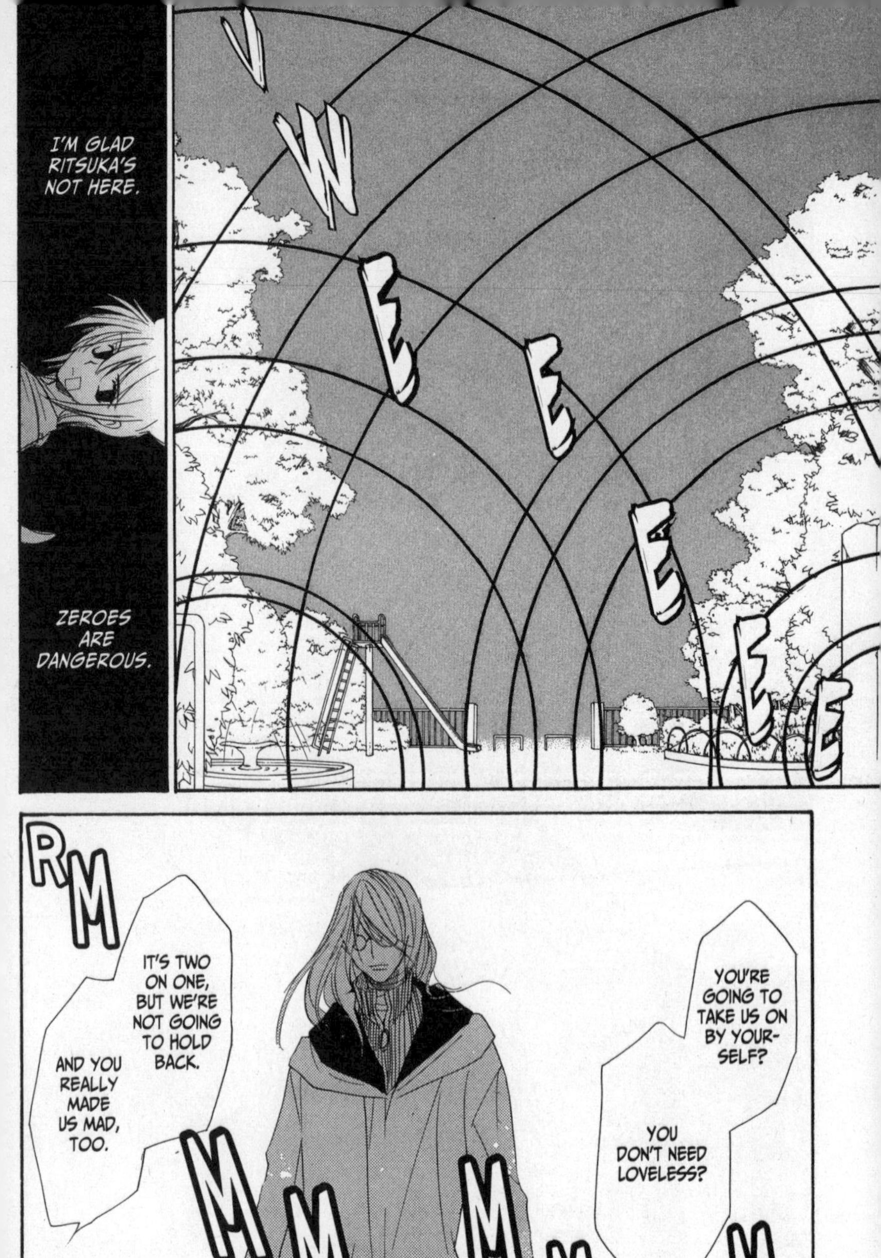
I'M GLAD RITSUKA'S NOT HERE.
VWEEEEEE
ZEROES ARE DANGEROUS.
RMMMMMMM
YOU'RE GOING TO TAKE US ON BY YOURSELF?
YOU DON'T NEED LOVELESS?
IT'S TWO ON ONE, BUT WE'RE NOT GOING TO HOLD BACK.
AND YOU REALLY MADE US MAD, TOO.

WITH A DIFFERENT NAME, YOUR POWER IS HALVED.

AND WITHOUT A SACRIFICE, YOUR POWER IS HALVED AGAIN.

YOU STILL WANT TO TAKE US ON?

BE GENTLE WITH ME.

YOU REALLY ...
...PISS US OFF !!
VWEEEN
SUPER PISSED!

Second District Park
WE'RE GOING TO TEAR YOU TO BITS.

ZZRRT
ZZRRT
ZZRRT
PSHAK
WATCH OUT FOR THE...
...HIGH VOLTAGE CURRENT.
OUR NAME IS ZERO.
WE ARE THE BEGINNING AND THE END.
WE ARE EVERY-THING.
AND NOTHING.
SHATTER.

WE SHALL GIVE YOU PAIN AND SUFFER-ING.
WE SHALL REDUCE YOUR EXISTENCE TO NOTHING.
WHAT...
...A NICE PHRASE.
"REDUCE MY EXIS-TENCE TO NOTHING."
WAS IT?
HWOOO
I LIKE THAT.
A LOT.

WOO
SH
A
KN
ZZRT
ZZRT

I SEE.
THEY'RE FAST...
RE-LEASE!
CON-DENSE!

RELEASE.
I HEARD THAT YOU'VE GOT...
...A HIGH PAIN TOLER-ANCE.
CON-GEAL!
DISSOLVE THESE BONDS.
SOLIDIFY INTER-NALLY.

VWOOO
I DON'T THOUGH.
I WONDER.
LET'S FIND OUT!

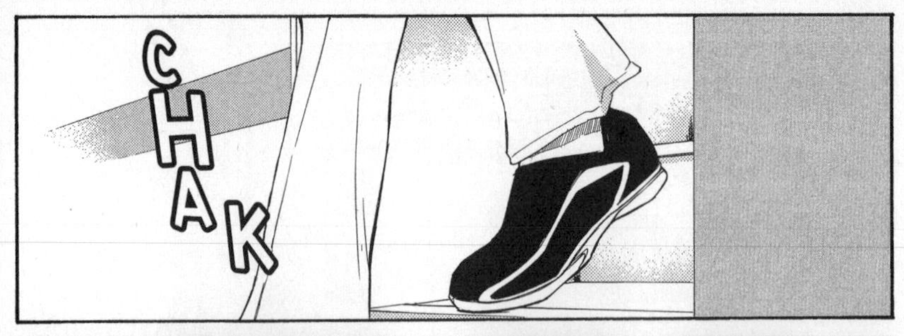

VROOOOM...

DR. KATSUKO INVITED ME ON A DATE THE OTHER DAY.

BUT...

WE HAVEN'T GONE YET.

I WANT TO GO. I WANT TO MAKE MORE MEMORIES.

MEOW

TBC!

loveless

●IN THE SUMMER 1/2●

FOLLOW YOU

HELLO. I'M KIO KAIDOU. (YEAH, I KNOW. IT'S A WEIRD NAME.)
REEE
REEE
...
REEE
TODAY I'M STALKING A GRADE SCHOOLER.

KIO.
YOU WANT A BEER?
OOPS, MY MISTAKE.
I'M JUST TAGGING ALONG WITH A PERVERT.

MAKE IT ICE COLD.
AND I'D LIKE A TUNA SKEWER.
THIS GUY IS SOUBI AGATSUMA (AGE 20).

WERE YOU KEEPING AN EYE ON RITSUKA AND THE OTHERS?
IT'LL BE A HASSLE IF WE LOSE THEM.
HE'S A TOTAL STALKER.

I'M WATCHING.
THIS GUY IS A PEDO FREAK WHO'S OBSESSED WITH A SIXTH GRADER.
I THINK THEY'RE OVER THERE BUYING JUICE.
SOU, WHY DON'T YOU STOP THIS?
JUST GO UP TO RITSUKA AOYAGI AND ASK TO PLAY WITH HIM.
HE'S DITCHING ME.
HEH
HE WANTS TO MAKE MEMORIES WITH HIS FRIENDS.
I CAN'T THIS TIME.
LAST NIGHT HE WARNED ME OFF.
HMM...
DO I REALLY HAVE NOTHING BETTER TO DO WITH MY SUMMER VACATION? ★

BUT IF IT WEREN'T FOR THIS KIND OF THING...
...SOUBI WOULD BE A PRETTY FINE CATCH.

HE'S TALL, AND HIS LOOKS AREN'T BAD.
AND ABOVE ALL, HE'S A TALENTED ARTIST. IT'S STARTING TO GET ON MY NERVES, TO BE HONEST.

ON THE OTHER HAND...
IF IT WEREN'T FOR THIS, HE MIGHT AS WELL HAVE BEEN A WALKING CORPSE.

BEFORE HE MET RITSUKA AOYAGI...

...HE WAS LIKE A ZOMBIE.

AAH.

LOOK.

LOOK, KIO.

THEY'RE GOING TO RIDE THE COSMO CLOCK.

AGH, NO WAY!!

I'M SCARED OF FERRIS WHEELS.

WHY?

THEY SHAKE!! YOU COULD FALL!!

OH.

YOKOHAMA

THAT'S TRUE.

IT *IS* SCARY.

LIAR.

THAT LOOK IN YOUR EYES SAYS YOU'RE NOT AFRAID OF ANYTHING RIGHT NOW.

AHA.
HE'S CHECKING HIS EMAIL.
HEH
TOO BAD. I'M NOT SENDING YOU ANY TODAY.

IF YOU WANT TO GO TO HIM, GO.
YOU'RE SO STUBBORN.

BUT YOU SEE, KIO...
I'M WAITING. I'M NOT RUSHING THINGS.

I'LL MAKE MY MOVE AFTER RITSUKA GETS A GOOD TASTE...
...OF WHAT IT'S LIKE TO BE WITHOUT ME.

YIKES, THAT'S YOUR GAME?
IS THAT SOMETHING YOU DO TO A GRADE SCHOOLER? YOU CREEP!
YOU'RE QUITE PECULIAR YOURSELF, KIO, TAGGING ALONG WITH ME.
WELL, *EXCUSE* ME!

NO, I APPRECIATE IT.
THANKS. YOU'RE MY BEST FRIEND.

YOU'RE ...
...WELCOME.

WAAAH, THAT WAS SO SCARY!

HOW CAN YOU BE SCARED OF HEIGHTS WHEN YOU'RE SO TALL, YUIKO?

EVEN IF YOU'RE TALL, SCARY THINGS ARE SCARY.

...HUH?

HUH?! WHAT?!

What are you doing here?

loveless

Yawn

IN THE SUMMER 2/2

STAND BY ME?

WHAT I KNOW ABOUT HIM:
1. HE'S AT THE SAME SCHOOL AS ME, BUT IN A DIFFERENT CLASS.
2. HE'S SHORT.
3. HE HAS A GIRLY NAME.
AND...

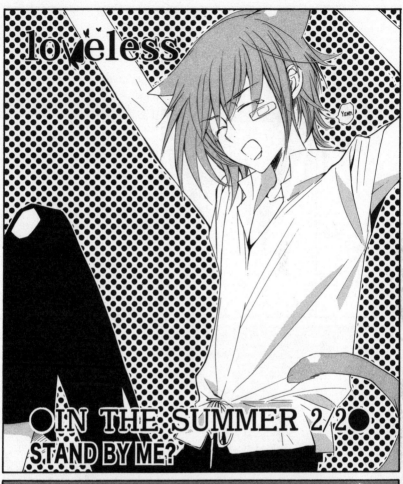

HE'S IN LOVE WITH YUIKO.
YOU'RE PRETTY GIRLY, AREN'T YOU?

(YOU'RE REALLY ONE TO TALK, I THOUGHT.)

SUMMER'S ALMOST OVER.

I'M MAKING MEMORIES.

IT'S HOT.

I'VE NEVER BEEN TO YOKOHAMA BEFORE! OOH, THE OCEAN!

IT'S WAY CLOSER THAN I THOUGHT!

IT'S REALLY FAST WHEN YOU TAKE THE TOYOKO LINE.

YUIKO, YOU SHOULD WEAR A HAT.

I DON'T LIKE HATS. MY EARS GET SWEATY.

HEY, SOU. EVEN JUST STALKING GRADE SCHOOLERS...

...IS STILL A CRIME.

YOU THINK?

WELL...

...LAST NIGHT...

I'M GOING OUT TOMORROW TO MAKE SOME MEMORIES.
OKAY. WHERE ARE WE GOING?
WITHOUT YOU, SOUBI!
MEANING?
I'M GOING TO YOKOHAMA WITH MY FRIENDS!
I CAN'T HAVE YOU ALWAYS HANGING AROUND ME.
IS THAT SO?
HISS!
YES, IT'S SO!!
ALL I HAVE ARE PICTURES WITH YOU.
THAT'S NO WAY TO MAKE A COLLECTION!

WHAT?
WHAT IS IT?!
NOTH-ING.
SMILE
THAT'S OKAY, YOU DON'T HAVE TO TAKE ME.
IF IT'S OKAY, THEN DON'T SAY IT LIKE THAT.
RITSUKA...
YOU'RE STILL JUST A CHILD.
B-BMP

YOU DON'T UNDERSTAND YET.

THAT THE MORE YOU SPEND TIME AWAY FROM ME...

...THE MORE YOU THINK ABOUT ME.

SILENCE

STARE

WHAT'S WITH HIM?

I WAS SURE THAT HE WOULD SEND ME SOME WEIRD EMAIL...

...OR TRY TO MESS WITH ME.

GOT A MES-SAGE?

UH, NO...

It's freaking me out.

IT'S HOT, ISN'T IT?!
I'LL GO GET SOME MOMI TEA!! SOME COLD ONES! ♡
WAIT HERE, GUYS!

H-HEY!
I'LL GO TOO, YUIKO!
THAT'S OKAY, I'M FINE.
La!
YOU GUYS CAN PLAY. ♡
EASIER SAID THAN DONE!!

THREE OF THEM?
GOT IT OKAY?
ER, I'M FINE!!
RITSUKA'S MAKING MEMORIES.
TODAY YAYOI CAME TOO.
I WANT TO RIDE THE FERRIS WHEEL.
I'M GONNA TRY TO MAKE THIS WORK!!
OOF!
OOF!
I HAVE TO TAKE LOTS OF PICTURES!
HEEEEY!
I'LL DO ANYTHING...
HERE, MILK TEA FLAVORED.
YOU LIKE THAT, RIGHT, RITSUKA?
I DO.
WHAT?
IT'S GOT SOFT CHEWY STUFF INSIDE.
DRINK UP!
...IF IT'S FOR RITSUKA.

HEY, THIS ONE'S RED BEAN MILK.
That's mine.
WOW, THAT LOOKS GOOD.
YOU WANT A TASTE?
SURE.
HEY!
HE DRANK IT.
HM?
UH...
I MEAN...
YOU GUYS GET ALONG WELL.
HUH?
SLRRRP
?
I GUESS.
You can try it too.
CLICK

KREE
KREE
KREE
KREE
...
...
...

IT...
IT REALLY...
KREE
KREE
IT ROCKS A LOT MORE THAN I EXPECTED.
YAYOI!
DON'T MOVE!
IT'S ROCKING.
KREE
IT'S ROCKING!
KREE
DON'T WORRY! WE WON'T FALL!
WE COULD FALL?!
W-WE'RE FINE. IF WE DO FALL, IT'LL BE OVER FAST.
SWOOSH
...
What a lame conversation.

KREE
I DIDN'T REALIZE IT WHEN I WAS LOOKING UP FROM THE GROUND ...
WOO
KREE
WOOOOOO
THE WIND'S REALLY STRONG WHEN YOU'RE HIGH IN THE SKY.
KREE
IT'S BEAUTIFUL.

I WISH...
...THAT SOUBI...
...COULD SEE IT.

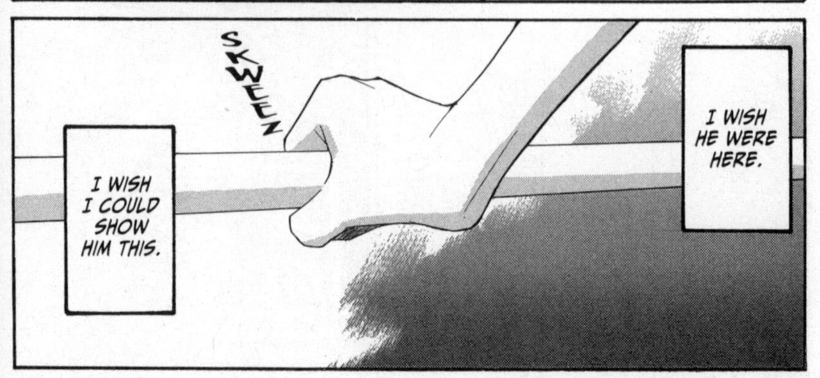
SKWEEZ
I WISH HE WERE HERE.
I WISH I COULD SHOW HIM THIS.

WAH, THAT WAS SO SCARY!
NO MORE FERRIS WHEELS!
HUH.
YOU'RE SO TALL, YUIKO, AND YOU'RE SCARED OF HEIGHTS?

I'M NOT THAT TALL!!
RITSUKA!!
How mean!
HUH.

EVEN IF YOU'RE TALL, SCARY THINGS ARE SCARY.
FLICK

NO WAY...

WHAT...
...ARE YOU DOING HERE?

DIDN'T YOU CALL ME?
WHA...
OF COURSE NOT!!
IT'S SOUBI! HELLO! ARE YOU AFRAID OF HEIGHTS?! ♡
OH, VERY AFRAID. ♡
DOING WELL, YUIKO?
EEE! EEE!
YAY!
I'M GREAT!
WHAT A FAKER!
NOTHING...
...SCARES YOU.
I CAN SEE IT IN YOUR EYES.

WOW, WHAT ARE YOU DOING HERE?
SMILE
IT'S QUITE THE COIN-CIDENCE.
That's a...
...lie.
LET'S GO, RITSUKA.
TUG
HUH?
YOU WANT TO RIDE ON THE FERRIS WHEEL, RIGHT?
I JUST GOT OFF IT...!
I did too!
LET'S GO AGAIN.
THIS IS WHAT HE WANTED TO DO?
WHAT A WEIRDO! WEIRDO!

CLICK

SINCE WE'RE IN YOKOHAMA, DO YOU WANT TO EAT IN CHINATOWN?

Just imagine that the moneybags are tagging along.

YOU THINK YOU CAN BARGE IN?

WHO INVITED YOU?!

COME ON, RITSUKA.

SOU SAYS IT'S HIS TREAT.

...WHO ARE YOU?

!!

WHO IS HE?!

LOVELESS 2 / END

Loveless Afterword
This Just In! Yun Kouga Near Death!
Ugh, I feel sick.
Every month my editor sets up a schedule.
Whaaat? That's impossible!
No way!
I've only got four days to draw these color pages!
And only three days to make changes for the graphic novel!
No way! No way! No way!
GRR
GRR
But my complaints notwithstanding...
Heh heh heh.
If I do the color pages in two days...
...and the changes in one day, I can play!
Heh heh!
...I had a secret plan!
It took me five days for the color pages, and four days to make the changes.
SPLUT.
"Perhaps you overestimate yourself?"
...said my editor.
Don't I get a grace period?!
A grace period!
If we gave you a grace period, we wouldn't make the deadline!
But scheduling up to the last minute isn't good!
You can't trust me! You can't trust manga artists! Isn't that the most basic rule?!
I never said I trusted you.
A FLY USING A CELL PHONE

Come by and play! http:// www.kokonoe.com
Here's the official website.
It's been a year since I started drawing *Loveless.* And I think I've finally gotten used to Ritsuka and friends.
MEOW
RITSUKA
Sometimes I see them in my dreams.
But for some reason...
...in my dreams...
I see things I can't tell anybody about.
WHY!!
EEK!
For example...
Do you want to go to a hotel?
Whaaat?!
Thanks, Dream Soubi.
.....
Or...
There are nails and a hammer in me.
What's inside me?
Or this.
SOMETHING AWFUL, I'M SURE
But they're just dreams. They don't mean anything.
...
...
I wonder...
...what happened next...
SILENCE
FUTON
THIS
Now then, since I previously (in volume 1) made public my work paper, a certain group of my friends wanted some, so I've been sharing it around.
By the way...
My manga paper is special order.
Isn't this convenient, it's an original!!
It says, "For Use by Yun Kouga" on it.
It makes me draw three times faster!!
Sieg Zeon!
Well then, until volume 3, I bid you adieu!!
?

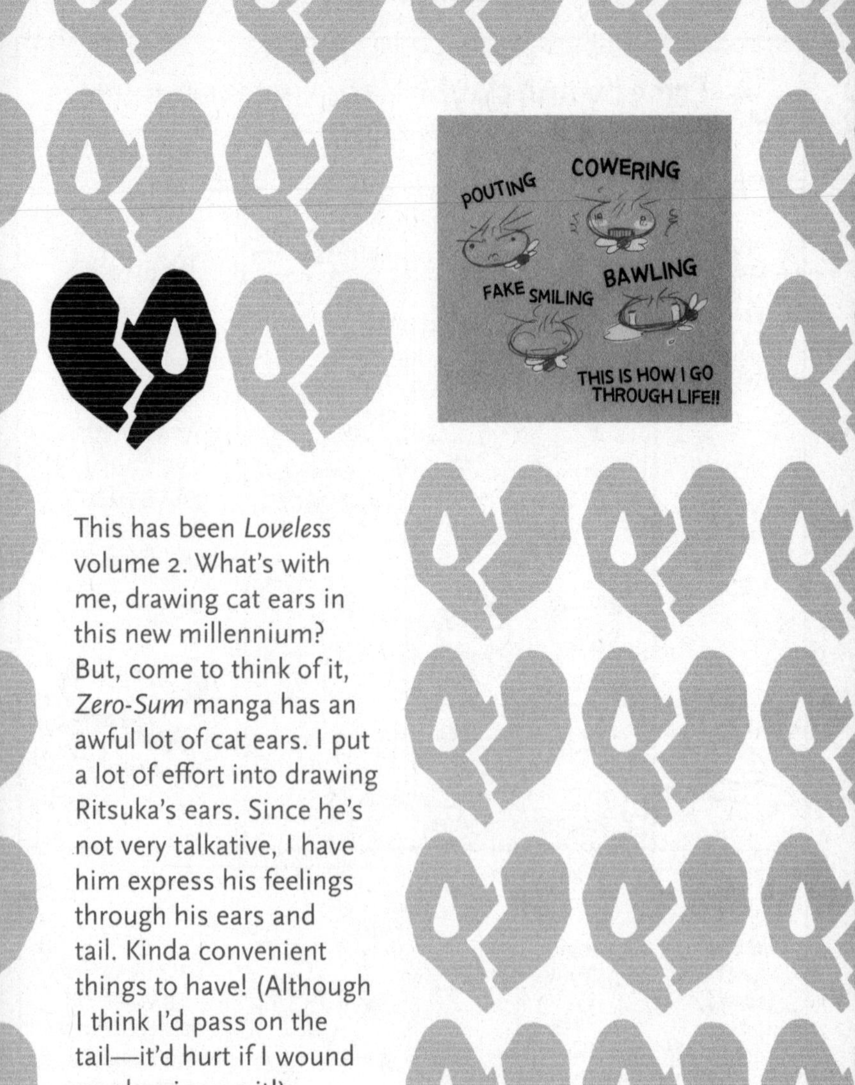
POUTING
COWERING
FAKE SMILING
BAWLING
THIS IS HOW I GO THROUGH LIFE!!

This has been *Loveless* volume 2. What's with me, drawing cat ears in this new millennium? But, come to think of it, *Zero-Sum* manga has an awful lot of cat ears. I put a lot of effort into drawing Ritsuka's ears. Since he's not very talkative, I have him express his feelings through his ears and tail. Kinda convenient things to have! (Although I think I'd pass on the tail—it'd hurt if I wound up sleeping on it!)

—*Yun Kouga, 2003*

(little loveless)

by Yun Kouga

AM I...
...AN EASY TARGET?
TRMBL
YES.
YES.
YES.
YES.
LOVELESS 2
TRMBL

WHY..
THE EASY-TO-AMBUSH TYPE
RITSUKA
MEOW
...ME?
Thank you for purchasing this special limited edition!! Off we go, into the world of loveless !

Injured and Unloved
loveless.

DOES A BODY GOOD♥

KAGOME
REFINING THE VEGETABLE
GOOD FOR ALL
VEGETABLES FOR LIFE!
DRINKABLE YOGURT
← VEGETABLE JUICE + DRINKABLE YOGURT

THAT KINDA ...
...LOOKS LIKE...
...VOMIT.
OH.
SLURP
I GUESS THAT'S TRUE!!

I'm sorry!!
Stop!
EWW!!
MROWR!
HA HA HA
DON'T SAY THINGS YOU'LL HAVE TO APOLOGIZE FOR LATER.
KAGOME VEGETABLES FOR LIFE DRINKABLE YOGURT IS DELICIOUS!!

I think it's a convenient, drinkable product.

ABOUT CHRISTMAS

I KNOW IT'S LATE TO BRING THIS UP, BUT I WAS THINKING... AFTER TAKING A DRIVE ALONG THE COAST AND HAVING DINNER AT A FANCY HOTEL...
...MAYBE WE'D SPEND THE NIGHT TOGETHER?
A LOREE RODKIN CROSS MIGHT MAKE A NICE PRESENT.
SPARKLE

OR MAYBE I SHOULD GO ALL OUT AND HEAD UP TO HOKKAIDO...
...FOR A REAL WHITE CHRISTMAS?
SPARKLE
NIGHT SKIING COULD BE NICE.
IT MIGHT BE ROMANTIC.

OMIGOD!
SOUNDS AMAZING!
I'M SO JEALOUS...
HEH
IT'S NOT THAT AMAZING.
AGATSUMA'S GIRLFRIEND IS SO LUCKY...
IF ONLY...
...IT WERE A GIRLFRIEND!!!

BUT I CAN'T. SCHOOL'S STILL IN SESSION ON THE 24TH.
AND DEPENDING ON HOW REPORT CARDS TURN OUT, WE MIGHT HAVE TO FACE SOME CRANKY PARENTS...
SIGH
WHAT ARE YOU SAYING?! OMIGOD!
SO DIRTY!
ARE YOU DATING A HIGH SCHOOL GIRL, AGATSUMA?!
...
IT'S AN ELEMENTARY SCHOOLBOY!!

My Christmas was just full of work.

THE DEVIL'S NUMBER

I NEED TO GET MY HAIR COLORED.
IT'S WINTER, SO MAYBE I'LL DARKEN IT A BIT.
YOU'VE GOT NICE COLOR, SOU.
WHERE DO YOU GET IT DONE? WHAT SHADE IS THAT?

THIS IS MY NATURAL HAIR COLOR.
FOR REAL ?!
SERI-OUSLY? LET ME SEE.

SHUDDER
SHUDDER
IT FIGURES !
IT FIGURES !!
WHAT DOES?
Not true.

Soubi is tainted, so ears don't suit him. 

A Conversation, to the Ends, Sans Underwear, and with a Toothache (and too long a title) !!!!

Kouga: Good evening!! I'm sleepy, so I have no idea what I'm going to write!! I'm the manga artist!

Sugino: ...Good evening! I'm in pretty bad shape too. I'm the editor, currently on the verge of saying something I shouldn't to my artist...

Ⓚ: (gets insult deja vu) GIGGLE! This time we worked even harder than before!

Ⓢ: Well, it's definitely been "hard" in terms of keeping quality, making quantity, and sticking to schedule... Yes, I mean that in a bad way, and yes, forget I said that.

Ⓚ: (is the better man) Master Sugi said just now, "You think you maybe put too much energy into drawing Kio?"

Ⓢ: Kio's the one who's most like you, isn't he, Ms. Kouga? And I've heard you say, "If I had to date anybody, it would be Kio..." So does that mean...?

Ⓚ: Who said that?! You're making that up!

Ⓢ: Birds of a feather. "Caregiver" + "likes dirty jokes" + "obsession with Chupa Chups." You see?

Ⓚ: (Eeeek!!) (Cats are being stuffed into clothes...) In any case, volume 2 is incredible.

Ⓢ: Incredible? I guess so. It IS incredible. At least the number of self-portraits you've included is. How many are there?

Ⓚ: An 800% increase over normal. This time, you see, I fine-tuned it like never before. I'm totally satisfied with this one!

Ⓢ: That's wonderful. I hope the readers are happy too. By the way, is that pork miso soup?

Ⓚ: It's cold soup over rice! After that bread I ate, I went for soup. *MUNCH MUNCH*

Ⓢ: Eat lots and grow up big and strong! You do cook quite a bit while you work, don't you...

Ⓚ: *MUNCH MUNCH* My assistants do the cooking. Sorry, I'm so hungry that I've been eating and writing at the same time.

Ⓢ: And there's nothing to talk about! I mean, all I can think of are sketchy things!

Ⓚ: Please cheer up. Please don't sleep in your car. Don't eat sukiyaki bento at dawn.

Ⓢ: It doesn't matter what happens to my body. But...perhaps drinking four liters of juice a day is extreme. And...you just keep eating.

Ⓚ: Always munch-a-lunching (I didn't have time to eat a real meal). By the way, do you realize Ritsuka's not wearing any pants in that illustration spread?

Ⓢ: Oh god, it's true! And he's only a grade schooler! But I guess age doesn't matter. But everyone in "little [illegible] loveless" is really cute.
(Oops.)

Ⓚ: No white-out... Please let me draw for little zero-sum as well! Ritsuka in little loveless seems to have a blushing problem.

Ⓢ: I'm sooorryyy (sob). Whatever happens, please keep hammering away and drawing your manga. Children blush a lot.

Ⓚ: People who blush easily are sexy, aren't they? It's like, what were you thinking just now?!

Ⓢ: But when KIDS blush it's because they're nervous! You just can't get your mind out of the gutter, can you? I bet you don't even blush.

Ⓚ: No, I don't. It's fine. Yes, it's fine. I've lost 5 kb. I made some tea. Drink it.

Ⓢ: You're fine? Uh...what's fine? By the way, what did you mean by "kb?" That's a mistake, right?

Ⓚ: (Can't you tell?!) ...hey, can I talk about...my tooth...really hurting.

Ⓢ: Your tooth?! That's terrible! Go to the doctor, or the hospital!! ...I mean, when you have the time. Yeah.

Ⓚ: Who are you trying to impress with that attitude? It'll be fine!! No toothache can win against my exhaustion!! Ha ha ha ha!!

Ⓢ: I worry about your pages. Why is Loveless always such an adventure? D:

Ⓚ: (It's like some strange musical instrument). It'll be fine!! Next time I'll draw Soubi without pants!! You'd think I was a pervert or something!

ROSY DAYS

by_Yutaka Kasami

Seimei told me that if he died, I was to go to Ritsuka. And Seimei died.

A master's orders are absolute. Disobedience is unthinkable; it cannot be done. When I heard these orders, as good as his last will and testament, I never dreamed they'd become reality. It was inconceivable, since a Fighter is almost always destroyed before a Sacrifice. But regardless of my own wishes, these prescient words became orders.

To Ritsuka I went.

These orders, a supreme honor for me, were simple in intent, but very difficult in execution. I operated under the assumption that Seimei wanted me to become Ritsuka's Fighter and thus protect him, because Seimei loved Ritsuka. A master's orders are absolute.

I agonized to death over how to best obey these orders. How would I approach Ritsuka? What if I barged into his house and announced that I was Seimei's Fighter? There were no indications that Seimei had told his family about himself. So naturally, the Aoyagi family, including Ritsuka, would not have been aware of my existence.

I decided Ritsuka would accept me more readily if I came into his life naturally. That would not include a proposition like, "Hey, little boy, you want to do something fun with me?" I'd be hauled off by the police.

As I was about to put my brush to Japanese paper, Kio called out to me.

"What do you want to do with this? Not like it has anything to do with you." *What a pain. If it doesn't have anything to do with me... Student teaching...?*

I grabbed the printouts from Kio's hands. According to the info from Seimei, Ritsuka was eleven years old, making him a grade schooler. This was the key!

"I didn't know you wanted to be a teacher," Kio edged. Thank you, Kio. It's good to have wonderful friends!

"Regarding grade school educational practices," the sheet read.

What fortune to have majored in Japanese art! If I had tried to student teach Japanese language or math, or if the grade level of the class to which I was assigned had been different, then I would have had no chance of ever meeting Ritsuka. But in an art class, I would have the chance to meet all of the children in all the grades.

So what class was Ritsuka in? To ensure that I didn't make a bad impression on Ritsuka, on the off-chance that we might cross paths unexpectedly, I began to smile all over the place and interact with the children every single day. Before that, my smile hadn't gotten much use, so my facial muscles were awfully sore. But I endured because I felt such ascetic training was a prerequisite for meeting Ritsuka. *Oh, Ritsuka, I want to meet you soon.*

One day, as I cleaned up the art classroom, a blushing little girl came up to me and asked, "Are you in love with anyone, Mr. Agatsuma?" I answered her, beaming, because I was. Someone I loved very much!

It was one week later when I discovered that Ritsuka had transferred to another school.

END

ROSY DAYS (part 2)

by_Yutaka Kasami

In order to fulfill Seimei's final orders, his last will and testament, I decided to make contact with Ritsuka. To ensure that Ritsuka would not dislike me, or not be overly cautious of me, I planned to meet him in a natural manner and talk to him naturally. Gradually he would open up to me, and afterwards...

My Happy Life Plan (some would call it wicked) went to pieces when Ritsuka transferred to another school in the aftermath of Seimei's death. I spent a hellish two weeks at that school without Ritsuka.

What meaning did my time as a student teacher have? I probably looked like the world was ending, even as the clamor of school went on around me. Kio was happy to point out the damage done when I returned to the university from my student teacher duties looking like I was at death's door.

"What happened, Sou? You look awful! Tell me everything."

I figured that if I told him that Seimei was involved, Kio might get angry, so I left that part out and gave a simplified explanation.

"Huh...? You want to know how to get to know a child in a natural fashion?"

Kio dropped his head into his hands and gave me a look like I was the biggest pedophile on earth asking him how to score a Lolita of my own. "I guess the most natural relationship would be between a student and cram school teacher, or if you were a school teacher..." Apparently, Kio's imagination wasn't willing to fly very far from home base on this one. So I was back to where I started, where people my age had no point of contact with children. So how to meet Ritsuka?

"What about becoming the cool older guy in his neighborhood?" Kio joked. I got the sense he was speaking about something from his own childhood. The friendly, responsible big-brother type from the neighborhood... What a great idea!

I could start with "Good morning, hello, isn't it a nice day? Do you need any help with your homework?" That seemed normal enough. That seemed natural. I didn't grow up in an environment where I could get to know "people in the neighborhood," so if someone said it was normal, I'd believe them.

It felt like it could work. I was sure Ritsuka would open up to me! I really had to hand it to my best friend Kio!

As I immediately set out buying real estate magazines, Kio said, "Don't go stalking a grade schooler now, okay?"

In case Ritsuka were to ever come over, I rented a one-bedroom apartment (bedroom and living room), a bit larger than a small apartment, near the Aoyagi residence, in accordance with the information I received from Seimei. The rent was a bit high, but a smaller apartment would have been too cramped, only big enough for a bed and TV. Besides, if I were to welcome him to a room with only a bed, Ritsuka would put his guard up and probably never come back again.

Since I had few possessions, moving was easy. The hard part was living. You ask what was the hardest part? Throwing out the garbage every day! Some things were combustibles, other things were recyclables, and on and on. Everything I bought, I had to sort out in my mind how to properly dispose of.

"Mr. Agatsuma, these are non-combustibles." I gave a strained smile to the meddling housewife who liked to examine every piece of trash I put out.

"I'm sorry. I'll be more careful." I could not afford to let Soubi Agatsuma's reputation drop before even meeting Ritsuka. The effort was back in my smiles. This time I hoped to finally meet Ritsuka!

It was one week later when I discovered that Ritsuka had not only transferred to another school, but had moved away as well.

END

STILL A PACIFIST

"I WILL NEVER USE VIOLENCE."
BLUSH
RITSUKA!! YOU'RE SO COOL! GOTTA HAND IT TO YOU, MY MASTER! ♥
LOVELESS 2 P.270

...BUT YOU KICKED THE DESK.
ON PAGE 245.
NO!
HISS
HISS
HISS
HISS
HISS
YOU DON'T GET IT!
THAT WAS FINE!
FINE?

IT'S FINE AS LONG AS YOU DON'T USE VIOLENCE AGAINST PEOPLE OR ANIMALS.
WHEN YOU DO IT TO INANIMATE OBJECTS, IT'S JUST TAKING YOUR ANGER OUT ON SOME-THING!
FWAP
LOVELESS 2
HMM...
I REALLY THINK THAT KICKING A DESK STILL COUNTS AS VIOLENCE.

HUH. WHAT-EVER.
MOVING ALONG. KISS ME.
ARGH!
WHY'D YOU JUMP STRAIGHT TO THAT?!

Whenever you run into a problem, solve it by saying "moving along."

loveless

FWAAAA

DU—H

RUSTL

IT'S GONE...

FWAAA
IT'S GONE.
GONE.
GONE.
I CAN'T FIND IT ANY-WHERE!!
WHAT SHOULD I DO?!
HOW COULD I HAVE LOST IT?
SHUF
SHUF
IT MEANT A LOT TO ME!!
SHUF
AND I JUST GOT IT TOO!!
SHUF

HERE.
A PRESENT FOR YOU, RITSUKA.
I MADE IT. WILL IT GET IN THE WAY AS A CELL PHONE CHARM?
NO.
SO YOU'LL KEEP IT?
YEAH.
YAY! I MADE ONE FOR SOUBI TOO.
SOUBI DOESN'T NEED ONE.
Doesn't deserve it.
WHAT?
HEY, YUIKO...

WHY DO YOU...
...GIVE ME THINGS?
HUH?
WELL, IT'S JUST STUFF.
ACTUALLY...
...I WISH I COULD GIVE YOU EVERYTHING, RITSUKA.
BUT...
...THIS IS ALL I HAVE TO GIVE.
AM I BEING ANNOYING?!
EEK!
NO, NOT AT ALL.
IT'S NOT THAT AT ALL.
Wow...
THANKS.
It's hand-made...!
I'LL TAKE GOOD CARE OF IT.

IT'S ONLY BEEN...
...ONE WEEK!
AGH, I CAN'T BELIEVE MYSELF.
I CAN'T REMEMBER WHERE IT IS!!
GRP
AND OF ALL THINGS, I STILL HAVE SOUBI'S.
AGH, I'M SO MAD!!
I HAVE TO FIND IT.
FIND IT. I HAVE TO FIND IT.
I CAN'T EVER TELL YUIKO THAT I LOST IT.
BUT WHERE DO I LOOK?!

RITSUKA!!
WHAT'S WRONG?
WHAT ARE YOU DOING?
URK!
MS. SHINONOME.
YOU DON'T EVEN HAVE AN UMBRELLA. YOU'LL CATCH COLD.
SPSH
DID YOU LOSE SOMETHING?
LOOK AT YOU, YOU'RE ALL WET...
WAS IT SOMETHING VALUABLE?
I'LL HELP YOU FIND IT.
WHAT IS IT?
...
IS IT A KEY?
TO YOUR HOUSE? OR YOUR BICYCLE?
IT'S OKAY.
MS. SHINONOME.
GUNG HO!
I'LL FIND IT BY MYSELF.
BECAUSE I WANT TO FIND IT...

IT'S REALLY ... ... REALLY ...

...IMPORTANT TO ME.

THE THINGS YUIKO GIVES ME...

...CAN NEVER...

...BE BOUGHT WITH MONEY.

AND TO LOSE SOMETHING LIKE THAT...

...IS UNFORGIVABLE.

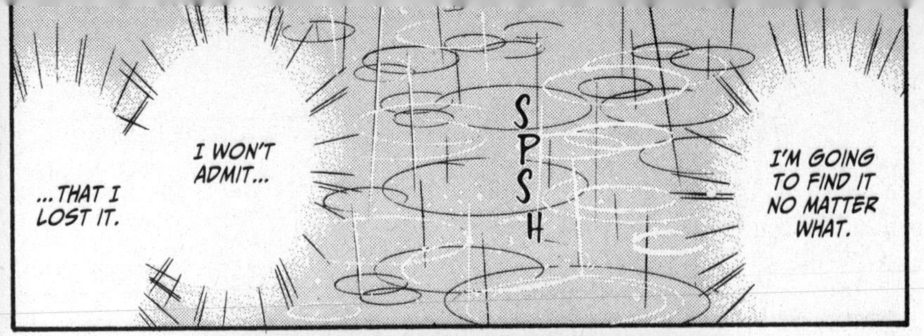

I'M GOING TO FIND IT NO MATTER WHAT.
SPSH
I WON'T ADMIT...
...THAT I LOST IT.

IF I CAN'T FIND IT...
SPLASH
...I'LL JUST DIE!!!

OH... OHH.

RIT-SUKA.

HE'S SO STUB-BORN.

HE'S STILL SEARCH-ING. WHAT SHOULD I DO?

SPSH SPSH SPSH

HE'LL GET SICK.

OH! I KNOW!

AT LEAST I CAN LEND HIM A RAIN-COAT.

HM?

FWAA

RITSUKA?
WHAT ARE YOU DOING?
Y...
AA AG H!!
PANIC!!
STOP IT, YOU'RE GONNA GET SICK.
ARE YOU LOOKING FOR YOUR CHARM?
ZING
WHA...
AGHH
...!!
AGHH
IT'S OKAY... YOU DON'T HAVE TO.
HERE.
CHK

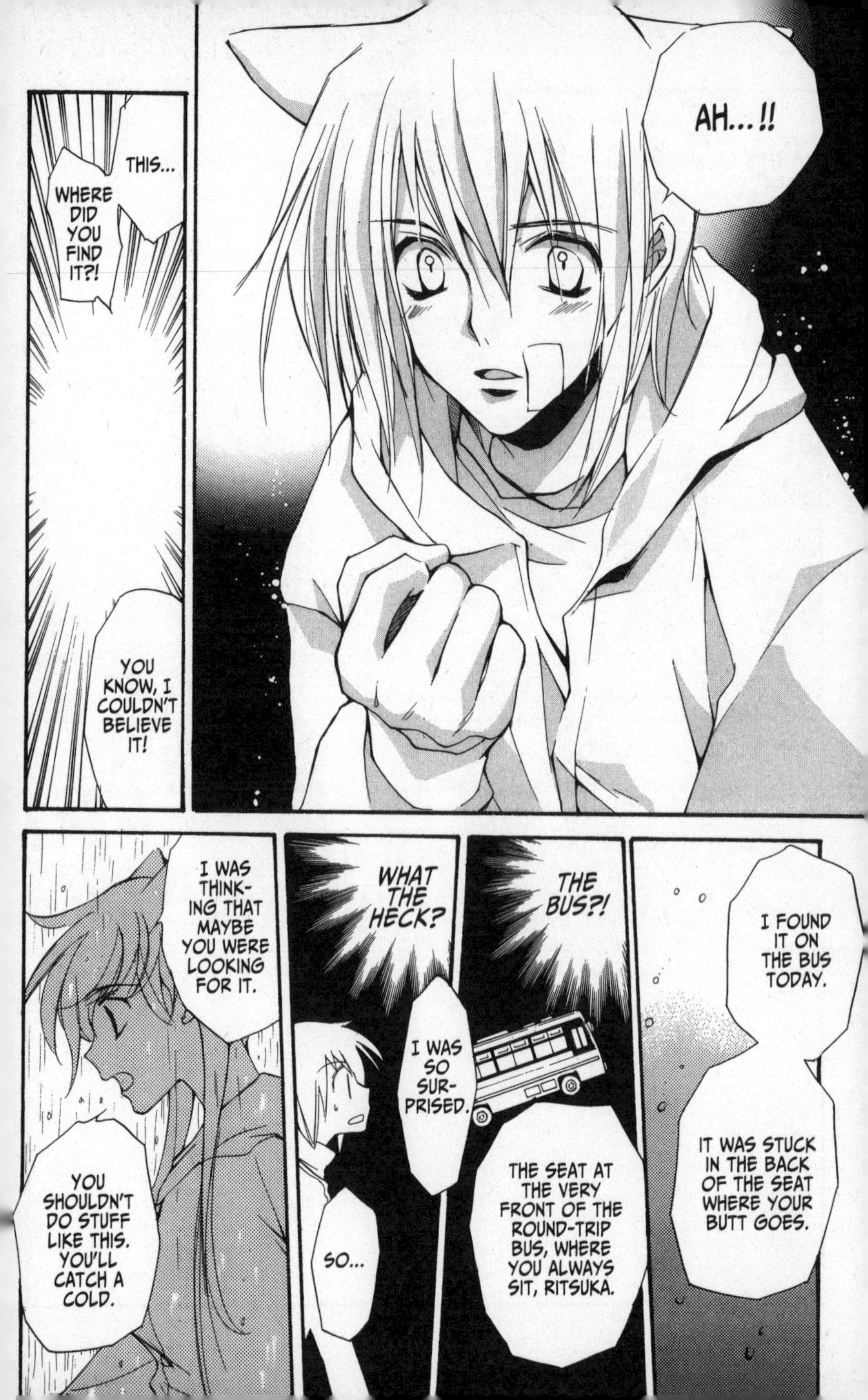

AH...!!

THIS...

WHERE DID YOU FIND IT?!

YOU KNOW, I COULDN'T BELIEVE IT!

I FOUND IT ON THE BUS TODAY.

IT WAS STUCK IN THE BACK OF THE SEAT WHERE YOUR BUTT GOES.

THE BUS?!

THE SEAT AT THE VERY FRONT OF THE ROUND-TRIP BUS, WHERE YOU ALWAYS SIT, RITSUKA.

WHAT THE HECK?

I WAS SO SURPRISED.

SO...

I WAS THINKING THAT MAYBE YOU WERE LOOKING FOR IT.

YOU SHOULDN'T DO STUFF LIKE THIS. YOU'LL CATCH A COLD.

THANK GOD YOU FOUND IT!

BUT...
I'M SORRY.
IT DOESN'T CHANGE THE FACT...
...THAT I LOST IT.

HUH?
THAT'S OKAY. DON'T WORRY ABOUT IT.
...
EVERYTHING BREAKS OR GETS LOST SOMETIME.
YOU JUST HAVE TO TAKE CARE OF IT UNTIL THEN!

little loveless 2 / END

loveless....
I've been into this style lately!!
I have such a thing for
eye-patches and syringes,
even though I hate hospitals.
yun k 2002-2003

THANK YOU VERY MUCH!!!

I put everything I know to use in creating this mini fan comic.

My apologies to anyone who didn't like it.

Ahh, I just love manga so much. I love it! I love it to death!! There's much, much more, so if you like, please stay along for the ride.

Guest Yutaka Kagami!! Thank you very much for your short, short stories with clever punchlines. Soubi was such a dork that I burst out laughing.

Yun Kouga,
2002 winter
→2003

SEE YOU SOON!

Total sexual harassment!!

1×2
END

began her career as a doujinshi author and debuted in 1986 with the original manga *Metal Heart*, serialized in *Comic VAL*. She is the creator of the popular series *Loveless* and *Earthian*, along with many manga and anime projects, including character design for *Gundam 00*. Her works *Crown of Love* and *Gestalt* are also published by VIZ.

Loveless

Volumes 1 + 2
VIZ Media Edition

Story and Art by YUN KOUGA

Translation // RAY YOSHIMOTO
English Adaptation // LILLIAN DIAZ-PRZYBYL
Touch-Up Art + Lettering // JAMES DASHIELL
Design // FAWN LAU
Editor // HOPE DONOVAN

Original Japanese edition published by ICHIJINSHA, INC., Tokyo.
English translation rights arranged with ICHIJINSHA, INC.

Printed in the U.S.A.

Published by VIZ Media, LLC
P.O. Box 77010
San Francisco, CA 94107

10 9 8 7 6 5 4 3
First printing, October 2012
Third printing, April 2015

www.viz.com